TO THE READER

This study guide is designed to prepare you for the Basic Skills Component of the Arizona Teacher Proficiency Examination. It is hoped it will eliminate the anxiety many people experience with this test. All new applicants for Arizona Teaching Credentials must take and pass this examination. The Basic Skills Component has 150 multiple choice items: 50 reading comprehension, 50 grammar, and 50 mathematics. The allotted time is four hours. Aids such as dictionaries and calculators are not permitted. Each skill area is graded **separately**; the minimum passing score in each skill area is 40 out of 50 questions (80%). The examination is offered on a regular schedule in Flagstaff, Phoenix and Tucson. For test registration information, contact:

ARIZONA DEPARTMENT OF EDUCATION
TEACHER TESTING UNIT
1535 West Jefferson
Phoenix, Arizona 85007
(602) 542-5414

This is a self-instruction study guide designed so you can learn at your own pace. If the material in a chapter is already familiar to you, take the Self-Test at the end of the chapter. If you do well, skip the chapter and go on to the next.

After each set of exercises, ask yourself *why* the answers were what they were and *what* you learned by completing these items.

Begin preparing for the test several weeks in advance. Provide yourself with a relaxed study environment and maintain a positive attitude.

What greater or better gift can we offer the republic than to teach and instruct our youth? — Cicero

A teacher affects eternity; he can never tell where his influence stops. — Henry Brooks Adams

ARIZONA TEACHER PROFICIENCY EXAMINATION

WORKBOOK

Primer Publishers
Phoenix, Arizona

ARIZONA TEACHER PROFICIENCY EXAMINATION WORKBOOK

By Diane Payne, B.S. Northern Arizona University, M.F.A. University of Arizona

Edited by George R. Fessler, M.A. in Education, Arizona State University

© 1995 by Primer Publishers
  4th Printing 1998
  Printed in the United States of America

Library of Congress Card Number TX1-390-813

ISBN 0-935810-52-8

All rights reserved. No part of this book may be reproduced in any form, by photostat, microfilm, xerography, or any other means, or incorporated into any information retrieval system, electronic or mechanical, without the written permission of Primer Publishers.

Primer Publishers
5738 North Central Avenue
Phoenix, Arizona 85012

TABLE OF CONTENTS

READING COMPREHENSION — 1

    Bridgeway Dispatch — 3
    Proposition 9 — 5
    Some Navajo Medicines — 8
    The Hummingbird and the Flower — 9
    Figurative Language — 14
    Synonyms, Antonyms, Homophones — 16
    Acronyms — 18
    Table of Contents — 19
    Interpret Charts — 20
    Alphabetical Order — 23
    Dictionary Skills — 24

MATHEMATICS — 25

    Addition and Subtraction of Fractions, Integers, and Decimals — 25
    Multiplication and Division of Fractions, Decimals, and Integers — 29
    Fractions to Percent, Decimals to Percent — 33
    Understanding Bar/Line Graphs — 35
    Word Problems — 36
    Averaging — 39
    Perimeter and Area — 40
    Liquid Measurements — 42
    Time Problems — 43
    Metric — 44

TABLE OF CONTENTS (continued)

GRAMMAR 47

    Periods, Question Marks and Exclamation Marks 47
    Comma for Clarity 49
    Common Prepositions 50
    Underlining Titles 53
    Hyphen 54
    Apostrophe-Possession 57
    Quotation Marks 59
    Colon 60
    Semicolons 61
    Use of Capital Letters 63
    Subject-Verb Agreement 67
    Verb Tense 72
    Pronoun Choice 75
    Possessive Pronouns 79
    Adverbs and Adjectives 81
    Sentences: Complete and Run-on 82
    Building/Changing Sentences: Subordinate and Invert 83
    Spelling 85

READING COMPREHENSION

Reading for answers on a timed test is a different realm than leisure reading. One way to develop better reading comprehension skills is to read material that is difficult for you. If you're not accustomed to reading a daily newspaper or current news magazines, try to include these in your everyday routine. Read the sections that you're not particularly interested in. What is required here is an ability to discern main and inferred ideas, subordinate details, cause and effect, sequence, inferred relationships and predict outcomes.

For some, vocabulary may be a problem. In preparation for the ATPE, whenever you come across a word you don't know, look it up. Keep a dictionary handy whenever you read. Make a flash card with the word on one side and the definition on the other. Try to incorporate these words into your conversations.

The passages in the ATPE test are not always interesting. Read the questions that go with the passages first; then look for the answers as you read. For practice, read the following questions first and then the passage which follows.

1. What was the area of Dr. Drew's major work?

2. What is meant by the word *difficulties*?

3. Why did Dr. Drew decide to devote his time to solving the problems of blood transfusion?

4. What is plasma?

5. In 1940 what was organized to aid war-torn France?

6. What is meant by the phrase "fallen into the hands of the enemy"?

7. Why did Americans give blood to help their British neighbors?

8. What is said in this story that makes you think more people survived injuries on the battlefield because of Dr. Drew's work in blood transfusion?

"Thousands of people are dying on the battlefields from loss of blood," said Dr. Charles Drew. "I must give my time to solving the problems of blood transfusion."

Physicians had studied blood transfusion for years. However, they had met with many difficulties because whole blood spoiled within days, and the matching of blood types was time-consuming. Nevertheless, Dr. Drew found there were fewer problems if plasma, instead of whole blood, was used in transfusion. Plasma, the liquid part of the blood without the cells, could be stored much longer and made the matching of blood types unnecessary. Anybody could be given plasma, and this was important on the battlefields of World War II.

In 1940 the Blood Transfusion Association set up a program for war-torn France. Dr. Drew asked them to send plasma rather than whole blood. But, it was started too late since France had fallen into the hands of the enemy.

Later, when Great Britain suffered heavy losses from air raids, Dr. Drew was asked to run a program called "Plasma for Britain." He organized the entire project, and thousands of Americans gave blood to help the British.

Without rereading the passage, see how many of the answers you can complete the first time around. Reread the passage to answer the rest. Check to see if your answers are correct.

Answers:

1. Blood transfusion — this question was looking for the main idea.

2. Problems — this question was interested in terminology.

3. Thousands were dying on the battlefields of World War II — this is an inference question.

4. The liquid portion of the blood without the cells — this is a fact.

5. Blood Transfusion Association — this is a fact.

6. France had lost battles to the enemy — this is terminology.

7. Britain has suffered heavy losses from air raids — this is inference.

8. Plasma could be stored longer; with plasma, blood typing was unnecessary — this is a conclusion-type question.

ATPE STUDY GUIDE

On this section of the test, it is important that you read both the questions and the passages carefully. What type of questions did you miss with the above exercise? If you missed the main idea questions, it would be useful to practice reading material that is providing the reader with information. After reading something, ask yourself, What was the author's purpose? Are you able to figure out the author's point? If not, reread it, underlining key points.

With an inference question you arrive at your conclusion by means of reasoning. Your reasoning should consider facts and consequences. The passage never directly stated that the Americans gave the blood to the British because they had suffered heavy losses from air raids, but this could be inferred from the information provided.

Fact questions are obviously seeking direct facts. We have already discussed ways to improve our vocabulary skills, so we need not indulge any further in the terminology-type questions. In the following exercises, try to read the passages more carefully, looking for the answers as you read.

Practice Paragraph Number 1: Bridgeway Dispatch

Directions: The following exercise is similar to a type the ATPE may use. Read the questions first; then read the following passage looking for the answers.

1. When she answered the ad for a photographer's assistant, Maria expected to receive:

    a. no reply.
    b. a rejection letter.
    c. an offer of employment.
    d. a request for a work sample.

2. When she first read the letter, Maria was:

    a. worried.
    b. satisfied.
    c. surprised.
    d. disappointed.

3. Mrs. Lester is Maria's:

    a. teacher.
    b. friend.
    c. mother.
    d. boss.

READING COMPREHENSION

4. The sentence about Maria's being tangled in a web of possibilities refers to her:

    a. difficulty in making a choice.
    b. interest in only one side of the problem.
    c. doubts about her ability as a photographer.
    d. feeling that she was trapped in her job as a checker.

5. Bridgeway is the name of:

    a. a distant city that is smaller than Fairharbor.
    b. a distant city that is larger than Fairharbor.
    c. a nearby city that is smaller than Fairharbor.
    d. a nearby city that is larger than Fairharbor.

6. If she buys a car, Maria will probably put off making a decision about:

    a. taking the job.
    b. saving her money.
    c. moving away from home.
    d. buying lots of clothes.

7. Fred's advice to Maria is similar to the old saying:

    a. Look before you leap.
    b. Home is where the heart is.
    c. Money doesn't grow on trees.
    d. A penny saved is a penny earned.

Maria answered an ad in the Bridgeway Dispatch *for a photographer's assistant, expecting to receive a form letter stating: "We appreciate your interest in our company. However, we regret to inform you...." She didn't expect anybody to want an assistant whose qualifications were two photography courses and a year's work checking groceries.*

Instead, the reply that arrived a week later was a large manila envelope containing a letter from Ms. Doris Chan, a memo entitled "Personnel Procedures," and an employment application. Also enclosed were the samples of her photography that Maria had sent with her letter and resume.

Maria read the letter twice to make sure Ms. Chan really did want her as an assistant. Her joy was soon replaced by worry. Was she a good enough photographer? Did she want to move away from Fairharbor and leave Mom,

Dad, and Fred? Would she feel lost in Bridgeway after growing up in a small town? How would she tell Mrs. Lester that she had to leave Famous Foods? On the other hand, the new job might mean a career in her chosen field. She could buy new clothes with the generous salary Ms. Chan's letter mentioned. And it would probably be good to live on her own and meet new people.

Maria was tangled in a web of possibilities when her brother, Fred, came home. Maria told him her thoughts. When she got to the part about all the clothes she could buy, Fred said, "Wait, Maria. Don't forget the expense of an apartment if you move to Bridgeway."

"I didn't think of that," Maria sighed. "What should I do?"

"What do you want to do?" Fred replied.

"Bridgeway's only twenty miles away," Maria mused. "I could buy a car and commute."

"Or you could cut down on expenses by getting a roommate," Fred offered. "What's most important is that you consider all the possibilities before you decide."

Maria smiled. "Thanks, Fred. I do want that job, but I guess no decision is easy. Buying a car might save me money if I continued to live here, but then I would just put off making another important decision that I think I'm ready to make. I'll sleep on it, but I'm pretty sure I know what I'll do."

Answers:

1. b, 2. c, 3. d, 4. a, 5. d, 6. c, 7. a

Practice Paragraph Number 2: Proposition 9

1. The author urges a "yes" vote on Proposition 9, primarily because the author feels that:

    a. the government has too much control over individuals.
    b. other, less expensive fuels must be found to replace gas.
    c. raising gas prices is the best way to protect valuable resources.
    d. raising gas prices will not solve consumption problems.

2. According to the passage, conservatives favoring the tax bill believe that raising gas prices will bring about:

   a. an increase in inflation.
   b. a further gas-price increase.
   c. a decreased demand for gas.
   d. an increase in the amount of gas available.

3. The author implies that if Proposition 9 is defeated, it is most probable that:

   a. wealthy people will buy larger cars.
   b. poor people will buy significantly less gas.
   c. demand for gas will stay relatively constant.
   d. all consumers will use fuel more thoughtfully.

4. The author's reference to "fuelishness" pertains to the:

   a. unthinking use of fuel.
   b. decreased supply of fuel.
   c. hoarding of fuel supplies.
   d. regulations governing fuel use.

5. According to the passage, an earlier apparent decrease in the supply of gasoline demonstrated mainly the:

   a. strength of the demand for gas.
   b. aggressive nature of the public.
   c. improper use of gas by the public.
   d. need for immediate higher gas prices.

6. According to the passage, the gas situation *cannot* be likened to the previous meat situation because:

   a. gas prices are regulated by the government.
   b. meat is perishable and cannot be stored like gas.
   c. meat supplies are more plentiful than gas supplies.
   d. meat and gas differ in importance to the consumer.

7. The "law of supply and demand" is:

   a. U.S. law governing the import of fuel.
   b. the law that would be repealed by Proposition 9.
   c. an economic principle that explains how consumers will act.
   d. the reason some consumers will steal to obtain scarce goods.

A vote for higher gasoline prices is not a vote for protection of natural resources. The recent bill that increased fuel taxes will not assure more gas in the future, but merely higher prices now.

The bill, which will become effective in three months, has received support from many conservative groups. They have urged citizens to vote "no" on Proposition 9, which calls for a repeal of this tax boost. They argue that Proposition 9 will allow drivers to continue their misuse of one of our most precious natural resources. This need not be so. Proposition 9 will not prevent future legislation designed to remedy our current "fuelishness." It will free us from an action that may prove costly in more ways than one.

What will happen if we do not repeal this move for higher gasoline prices? Opponents of Proposition 9 claim that drivers will use less gas when it becomes more expensive. They talk about the "law" of supply and demand, which refers to the interrelatedness of the supply, demand and price of a given product. If the supply of a product is fixed, or severely limited, an increase in demand will raise its price. When the price reaches a certain point, the consumer weighs the importance of the product against its inflated price. If money means more to the consumer than having the product, the demand decreases. Consequently, the price may return to a reasonable level.

Indeed, this happened when meat prices rose some years ago. Demand, and then price, decreased. We cannot liken this to our current situation, however. Those who are driving the least economical cars are also, for the most part, those who have the most money. They will not mind spending 10 or 20 cents more a gallon. Driving is a way of life for many in this country. They proved that several years ago by rising at 4:00 a.m., waiting in hour-long gas lines, cheating, and even stealing to obtain gasoline because they were led to believe the supply had been drastically reduced.

We must rely on the people, rather than the government, to handle the fuel crisis. Vote "yes" on Proposition 9 this Tuesday.

READING COMPREHENSION

Answers:

1. d, 2. c, 3. c, 4. a, 5. a, 6. d, 7. c

Practice Paragraph Number 3: <u>Some Navajo Medicines</u>

1. Which plant is used for colds, fevers and sugar diabetes?

    a. Mountain Mahogany
    b. Colorado Blue Spruce
    c. Bottle Brush
    d. Juniper

2. Which root is an important medicine for physical injuries, especially those injuries caused by horses?

    a. Prairie Clover
    b. Wild Buckwheat
    c. Silky Sophora
    d. White Evening Primrose

3. According to the story, what will happen to white people if they eat jei nayoogisii?

    a. They will become more sexually active.
    b. It will prevent appendicitis attacks.
    c. They will look thirty years younger.
    d. They will have a heart attack.

4. Which mountain is the female mountain?

    a. Black Mountain
    b. Chuska Mountain
    c. Mount Lemmon
    d. Mount Everest

Navajos know and use many herbs and other plants as medicines. Some of them are used in Navajo ceremonies; others are taken or used whenever they are needed. The medicinal herbs grow in different places, many of them on the sacred mountains. Some grow on high places, and some grow in the lower areas.

Black Mountain and the Chuska Mountain range grow many of the medicine plants. Black Mountain is the female mountain, and the plants which grow on it are female plants. The Chuska range is the male mountain, and the plants which grow on it are the male plants.

The Spreading Fleabane is used to ease childbirth. Pregnant women drink the potion prior to and until birth takes place. It also is used during the castration of horses so that the veins will heal properly.

The root of the wild buckwheat is an important medicine for physical injuries, especially injuries caused by horses. After an accident, the medicine should be eaten and applied on the victim. Then it should be put on the horse. This is a "Lifeway" medicine.

The Bottle Brush plant is found all over the reservation. Its root is boiled in water and the liquid is drunk by the patient. It is used for colds, fevers and sugar diabetes. The medicine is a "Lifeway" medicine and is used in the "Lifeway ceremony."

A harmful kind of cactus is called the "heart twister cactus" (jei nayoogisii). If a Navajo eats the cactus, it will twist his heart. If a white person eats it, he will have a heart attack.

Medicine plants are to be used with thanksgiving and are not to be wasted or ruined for fun. One must pray for the medicine plants before eating or using them. One also should make an offering to the plants with corn pollen. There are medicine plants for just about every condition or illness.

Answers:

1. c, 2. b, 3. d, 4. a

Paragraph Number 4: <u>The Hummingbird and the Flower</u>

1. When the hummingbird was first asked how she obtained such a beautiful dress, she said it was because:

    a. she had a good tailor.
    b. of the panther.
    c. of the mud.
    d. of the mouse.

2. <u>Colibri</u> means:

   a. fool.
   b. hummingbird.
   c. good grief!
   d. mouse.

3. The panther was unable to tell day from night because:

   a. time never changed.
   b. alligators rubbed mud in his eyes and sealed them with gum.
   c. they were so similar.
   d. the mouse sealed his eyes shut with gum and plastered over them with mud.

4. The <u>esteros</u> are the:

   a. arms of the sea at the mouth of a river.
   b. estrogen inside an alligator.
   c. mats surrounding a pond.
   d. lily pads.

5. The hummingbird thought the panther was wise because:

   a. he wanted the mouse killed.
   b. he travels a great deal.
   c. he was a large animal, and therefore must have a larger brain.
   d. he looked intelligent with gum and mud in his eyes.

6. The hummingbird picked the panther's eyes clean because:

   a. she hated seeing mud in one's eyes.
   b. she was a humanitarian.
   c. she wanted him to kill the alligator.
   d. she wanted to know how she could have a beautiful dress.

Read the questions first; then read <u>The Hummingbird and the Flower</u>.

"Good morning, pretty flower!"

"Good morning, little hummingbird!"

"May I have some honey, please?"

"Certainly. Here is plenty. Help yourself."

"Thank you. It is very good of you. Is there anything that I can do for you in return?"

"Well, I hear so little, seeing that I do not go abroad, that I love to be told things. I wish that you would tell me how you come to have so beautiful a dress. I have often wondered as I saw you flashing past."

"Have you indeed? Well, let me think. I believe I have heard that it was because of a mouse that I have it."

"A mouse? How can that be, busy little Colibri? A mouse, you know, is dull and gray."

"Then, Florecilla, if it was not a mouse, it was mud."

"My dear hummingbird, you must be wrong. You know as well as I do that mud is dull and gray. Won't you stop your humming a moment and think?"

"Ah, now I know. It was because of a panther."

"Dear, dear Colibri, that is worse still. A panther, did you say? I must have heard wrong."

"Isn't that right, either? Well, it must have been all three—the mouse, the mud and the panther. So there now.... But how sweet this honey is."

"Indeed, I am glad that you find it so. But please tell me about your pretty dress."

"Oh, yes. I forgot, thinking of the honey. One has so much to think of. I remember now, perfectly well. It was Paloma the dove who told me all about it yesterday, but a day and a night is a very, very long time to remember a long tale."

"Then tell me before you forget."

READING COMPREHENSION

"Well, once all hummingbirds were gray."

"So I have heard."

"Well, a big panther was going through the woods very quietly, and he stepped on a mouse nest and happened to kill all the baby mice."

"Dear me. I am so sorry to hear that."

"So when the mother mouse came to her home and saw what had happened, she was very much annoyed, saying that the panther was too big and too clumsy and did not look where he was going."

"Well, Colibri, she would be annoyed. You know I have often thought how nice it would be if mice and panthers and all creatures did not move about as they do. They run about so and they jump and skip, and it is no wonder that things happen. Suppose trees and flowers and bushes were as restless as animals. Think how it would be with great trees treading on little flowers, and thorn bushes running about and tearing down the gentle "flores del aire" and scratching the tender skins of the grapes. Now if I were queen, I would make a law so that all those forest creatures that run on four legs would just stand and grow as we do, and—"

"Please do not interrupt or I may forget the tale."

"Oh, I beg your pardon. Go on, please."

"Well, of course the panther told the mother mouse how it had happened and said that he was sorry and that he would be more careful, but she scolded him and kept it in her heart to punish him."

"But, little Colibri, if he said that he was sorry, and if it could not be helped, then it seems to me—"

"Really, little flower, you must listen. You have no idea how difficult it is to tell a tale. So please do not interrupt. One day, when the panther was asleep, the mouse crept up with some gum which she had taken from the tree and sealed up the panther's eyes. Then she took mud from the laguna and plastered it over the gum, and then more mud and more mud, so that the panther could not tell day from night."

"Dear me. That was very unkind and very dreadful. I am as sorry for the panther as I am for the mother mouse."

"Well, anyway, that proves that it was a mouse and a panther and mud, just as I said."

"But, dear hummingbird, how about the dress of many colors?"

"I am coming to that, but you interrupt so. The panther roared and roared and roared, until the very softest of his roars shook the "esteros", and the alligators were frightened and dived to the bottom of the water. Hearing all that noise, a hummingbird asked the panther what the noise was all about."

"That was very good of the hummingbird. And what did the panther say?"

"He told the hummingbird all about it and asked him to kill the mouse. But that the hummingbird would not do."

"Of course not. I never killed a mouse."

"So then the panther said that if the hummingbird would take away the gum and the mud so that he could see again, he would do anything that he could in return. You see, little flower, the panther is wise because he travels so much and all things that travel know a great deal."

"I am not so sure of that, Colibri. All this summer I have traveled up this tree and so have gone a great distance, but I know very little."

"That is different. No one wants a flower to be wise. To be beautiful is enough."

"Oh!"

"But please listen and do not talk so much."

"I am very sorry that I interrupted you, little hummingbird."

"Well, the hummingbird told the panther that she wished to have a beautiful dress, as beautiful as the dress of the sun bird, and asked him to tell her where she could get bright colors. Then before the Panther answered, she asked him to tell her how the "lianas" got the red and yellow and purple for their blossoms."

"This is the most interesting thing I have ever heard, and I hope the tale will not be short. Did the panther know?"

"Of course he knew. He told her that the flowers got their color from the earth, and he also told her where there was clay of many colors and where there were gold and silver and rubies. So the hummingbird picked and picked until the panther's eyes were unsealed and the big fellow gave a roar of gladness. All that day, panther and hummingbird worked, bringing colored clay and colored sands, and silver and gold, and rubies and opal, and the blue and crimson of sunset, and the silver of the moon and the stars, and the tender green of shady forests, and the blackness of ebony. Out of all these, the hummingbird dressed herself, and for misty-moving wings she took the spun silk of the spider and the soft thread of the "sumaha". And that is how the hummingbird got her dress. There now."

"I am glad to know that, dear hummingbird, and I thank you for telling me."

"And I, dear flower, thank you for the honey."

"Good-bye, then, if you must go."

"Good-bye, Florecilla.... B-z-z-z-z. H-m-m-m-m-m-mmmmmm."

This passage came from *Tales from Silver Lands* by Charles Finger.

Answers: 1. d, 2. b, 3. d, 4. a, 5. b, 6. d

FIGURATIVE LANGUAGE

Figurative language includes metaphors and similes. A **metaphor** is an implied likeness between things.

> Instead of studying a history assignment carefully, from beginning to end, George merely frogs through it.

A student and a frog are unlike things; but they have a link of likeness, provided by the verb frogs, in the way George leaps through his assignment.

Metaphors enable the reader to associate concrete images with the ideas presented. These images, if fresh and relevant, help him to understand and remember. For example:

> In the opening lecture, the professor spun his wheels for ten minutes before he began to move ahead.

In this metaphor, the writer finds a likeness between a professor and a car and uses it to vividly depict the professor's wasted effort before getting down to business in his lecture.

Metaphors are words that paint a picture. They are figures of speech. Consider the following:

>Joe's bark is worse than his bite.
>A fossil of a woman used to be our baby sitter.
>Poindexter is a walking encyclopedia.
>His heart is an iceberg, while hers is a fountain of kindness.

Obviously, none of these people are what the sentences really say.

Similes are a figure of speech in which two dissimilar things are compared by the use of *like* or *as*. Similes are usually a poetic or imaginative comparison.

>That man is like a fox.

We are comparing him to a fox, he is not a fox. A metaphor of the preceding example would be:

>That man is a fox.

Of course, he's not really a fox. Similes are words that describe by comparison.

drank like a fish	as stubborn as a mule
as quick as a wink	as dark as night
as light as a feather	as meek as a lamb
as thin as a rail	as soft as silk
as dry as a bone	as quiet as a mouse
as cute as a button	as clear as day

Try to incorporate original metaphors and similes in your writings. These are as worn out as an old shoe. Get my point?

Place an <u>S</u> for a simile and an <u>M</u> for metaphor before each sentence.

1. _____ To climb the ladder of success, you must leave no stone unturned.

2. _____ She ran like a deer.

3. _____ I got stuck in the mud with a math problem.

4. _____ The man is like a bovine.

READING COMPREHENSION

Answers:

1. M, 2. S, 3. M, 4. S

SYNONYMS, ANTONYMS, HOMOPHONES

Synonyms are words having the same, or nearly the same, meaning.

Antonyms are words that are opposites, or nearly so.

Homophones are words which agree with each other in sound, and perhaps in spelling, but differ in meaning.

SYNONYMS

day, date, occasion	make, build, construct
place, put, arrange	work, labor, toil
think, consider, believe	find, locate, retrieve
call, shout, summons	time, period, season
carry, tote, lug	grab, steal, take
eat, dine, devour	idea, thought, concept

ANTONYMS

on, off	all, none	near, far
work, play	alive, dead	back, front
add, subtract	hot, cold	good, bad

HOMOPHONES

air, heir	allowed, aloud	aisle, I'll, isle
altar, alter	carat, carrot	arc, ark
ate, eight	board, bored	cell, sell
bail, bale	boy, buoy	cent, scent, sent
be, bee	brake, break	cheap, cheep
bare, bear	bread, bred	chews, choose
fir, fur	flea, flee	feat, feet
dew, do, due	flour, flower	principle, principal
rap, wrap	passed, past	mall, maul
tail, tale	shone, shown	rude, rued
we, wee	vary, very	weak, week

ATPE STUDY GUIDE

Some dictionaries provide antonyms and synonyms for words. A thesaurus also shows synonyms. Your reading comprehension skills will develop as you familiarize yourself with more words.

The ATPE may provide questions like this:

Choose the word that means the *opposite* of the underlined word.

1. the probable cause

    a. obvious
    b. natural
    c. sensible
    d. unlikely

2. to be proficient

    a. quiet
    b. inept
    c. respected
    d. unfortunate

Answers: 1. d, 2. b

Here is another type of question you may encounter.

1. The following words, not and knot, are:

    a. antonyms
    b. homophones
    c. synonyms
    d. metaphors

2. The following words, blue and blew, are:

    a. antonyms
    b. synonyms
    c. homophones
    d. similes

Answers: 1. b, 2. c

Choose the word that has about the *same* meaning as the underlined word.

1. to start the ball rolling

    a. begin
    b. survive
    c. retaliate
    d. stand aside

2. the most valuable commodity

    a. catalog
    b. customer
    c. merchandise
    d. salesperson

3. to gain jurisdiction

    a. revenge
    b. authority
    c. experience
    d. justification

Answers: 1. a, 2. c, 3. b

ACRONYMS

Acronyms are the initials of words used together. People usually read these as words:

AIDS	Acquired Immune Deficiency Syndrome
AWOL	Absent without Leave
BASIC	Beginners All-purpose Symbolic Instruction Code
BMOC	Big Man on Campus
GASP	Group Against Smoking in Public
HUD	Housing and Urban Development
NASA	National Aeronautics and Space Administration
NATO	North Atlantic Treaty Organization
NOW	National Organization for Women
RIP	Rest in Peace
UFO	Unidentified Flying Object
VISTA	Volunteers in Service to America
WHO	World Health Organization

TABLE OF CONTENTS

The Table of Contents is found in the front of a book. Its purpose is to inform the reader of the book's contents (what the book covers). The Table of Contents tells you what pages each chapter covers, the sequence of information, and the emphasis and relationship of parts. It is similar to an outline.

Let's take a look at a Table of Contents:

Unit I

Lesson 1.	Words from Proper Names	1
Lesson 2.	Appearances and Attitudes	6
Lesson 3.	Words About Groups	10
Lesson 4.	Sounds Italian	15
Lesson 5.	Jobs and Professions	20
Lesson 6.	Mythology	25
Lesson 7.	Social Sciences	30

The ATPE may ask questions related to the Table of Contents like the following:

1. From which Lesson could you find information regarding words like: *libretto, salvo, adagio, bravura*?

    a. Lesson 1
    b. Lesson 4
    c. Lesson 2
    d. Lesson 5

2. From which Lesson would you find information regarding words like: *Adonis, Cupid, Olympian, Odyssey*?

    a. Lesson 1
    b. Lesson 7
    c. Lesson 6
    d. Lesson 2

The answer to Question #1 is *b*. The words are all Italian. The answer for Question #2 is *c*, as all the words are related to mythology.

For practice, it may be a good idea to look through some textbook Table of Contents to see what it relates to. People sometimes get the Index confused with the Table of Contents. Indexes are in the back of the book, listing individual words which can be found on certain pages in the book. Table of Contents describe the chapter.

INTERPRET CHARTS

In order to interpret charts correctly, you must read them carefully. An example that may be on the ATPE is similar to the following:

Directions: Use this paycheck stub to answer questions 1-3.

PERIOD ENDING 01-10-99		EMPLOYEE NUMBER 527-00-0000		DATE OF CHECK 01-13-99	
TYPE OF EARNINGS	CURRENT	YEAR TO DATE	TYPE OF DEDUCTION	CURRENT	YEAR TO DATE
REGULAR	150.00	300.00	FEDERAL INCOME TAX	16.71	33.42
			FICA TAX	9.10	18.20
GROSS EARNINGS	150.00	300.00	TOTAL DEDUCTION	25.81	51.62
			NET THIS CHECK	124.19	

1. How much has the employee earned so far this year?

    a. $124.19
    b. $150.00
    c. $300.00
    d. $450.00

ATPE STUDY GUIDE

2. The "total deductions" are:

   a. added to the gross earnings.
   b. subtracted from the gross earnings.
   c. subtracted from the net earnings.
   d. collected when the employee files a tax return.

3. How much money did the employee receive when cashing the check attached to this stub?

   a. $ 51.62
   b. $124.19
   c. $150.00
   d. $300.00

Answers:

1. *c.* To find the answer to number one, you need to realize the "gross earnings" are the total earnings before anything has been deducted. The employee has earned $300.00 so far this year. He currently earned $150.00, but overall this year he has earned $300.00. The "current" amount represents the paycheck for one pay period.

2. *b.* The "total deductions" are subtracted from the "gross earnings." The "net pay" is the amount left after the deductions have taken place. The "total deductions" for the pay period is $25.81 subtracted from $150.00, which gives us the "net pay" of $124.19.

3. *b.* When the employee cashed the check, the "net pay" was $124.19.

Here is another practice visual:

Directions: Use these lists of ingredients of four varieties of mayonnaise to answer questions 1 and 2.

> First survey each list, noting differences in ingredients. Then answer questions.
>
> **Brand 1:** liquid safflower oil, liquid soybean oil, whole eggs, water, vinegar, egg yolk, lemon juice, mustard seed, flour, paprika.
>
> **Brand 2:** water, soybean oil, modified food starch, egg yolk, vinegar, salt, whole egg, mustard flour, sodium benzoate and calcium disodium EDTA as preservatives, natural and artificial flavors, oleoresin, paprika, artificial color.

Brand 3: vegetable salad oil, whole eggs, vinegar, water, egg yolks, salt, sugar, lemon juice and natural flavors, calcium disodium EDTA added to protect flavors.

Brand 4: soybean oil, eggs, water, vinegar, salt, sugar, lemon juice, mustard, flour, paprika, natural flavors, calcium disodium EDTA to protect flavor.

1. Which brand does *not* contain preservatives.

    a. Brand 1
    b. Brand 2
    c. Brand 3
    d. Brand 4

2. Which brand could be eaten by a person on a salt-free diet?

    a. None of the brands
    b. Brand 1
    c. Brand 2
    d. Brand 3

Answers:

The correct answer to question number one is *a*. One needs to know that calcium disodium EDTA is a preservative. Brand 2 states that calcium disodium EDTA is a preservative; brands 3 and 4 don't mention that fact. Careful reading is a must to interpret these charts correctly.

The correct answer for question number two is *b*. Brand 1 is the only list that doesn't include salt in the ingredients. A salt-free diet means one that doesn't have salt.

Directions: Use these directions from medicine bottles to answer questions 1 and 2.

BUFFER-GEL — For upset stomach take 2 teaspoonsful every 2 hours; or take after meals and at bedtime. Do not exceed 20 teaspoonsful per day, or as directed by a physician. Do not use maximum daily dosage of this product for more than 2 weeks. Not to be used by persons having kidney disease or those on a sodium-restricted diet, except under the advice and supervision of a physician. Do not take with antibiotics.

TUMEZE   Take 1 teaspoonful every 4 hours or as directed by a physician, not to exceed 5 teaspoonsful in 24 hours. If stomach pain or nausea persists, a physician should be consulted.

1. According to the directions, one should *not* take two teaspoonsful of BUFFER-GEL:

    a. before bedtime.
    b. twelve times in one day.
    c. for more than a week.
    d. after breakfast or lunch.

Answer:

The correct answer is *b*. The directions for BUFFER-GEL limit the dosage to 2 teaspoonsful no more than 10 times a day.

2. The user is advised to consult a doctor if TUMEZE does not stop stomach pain or nausea. This warning is included because:

    a. the dosage might have to be increased.
    b. the user might not be following the directions.
    c. the user may be immune to the effects of TUMEZE.
    d. the user might have a problem that should be treated by a doctor.

Answer:

The correct answer is *d*. Once again, the answer is not stated directly in the directions, but it is implied. The other choices may be possibilities for reasons one may still have stomach pain or nausea, but the best answer would be to have the problem treated by the doctor.

ALPHABETICAL ORDER

To place something in alphabetical order, you must break the word down letter by letter. Let's say you are asked to alphabetize the words: green, groan, grunt. Which word would come first? Green, because the letter *e* comes before *o* and *u*. The correct order would be: green, groan, grunt.

Place these words in the correct order: numerous, numerator, numerical, number.

_____   _____

_____   _____

The correct order is: number, numerator, numerical, numerous.

The ATPE may ask you a question like this:

1. Consumer Carburetor's supply catalog would be filed between the catalogs of:

    a. American Mufflers and Dawson Motors
    b. Dawson Motors and Flash Motor Co.
    c. Roderick's Road Supply and Speed Shop, Inc.
    d. Flash Motor Co. and Griffen Exhaust Systems

    The correct answer is *a*.

DICTIONARY SKILLS

Put a dictionary next to you as you do these exercises.

1. The word *headstone* would be found between which entries?

    a. heat engine — heighten
    b. headlock — heatedly
    c. haulage — headline
    d. harm — haul

    The answer is *b*.

2. The word *ornery* would be found between which entries?

    a. optical — ordinary
    b. ope — optic
    c. ordination — oscillate
    d. oscillation — outdistance

    The answer is *c*.

Alphabetizing, using more than the first letter, is how you find the correct answers.

ATPE STUDY GUIDE

MATHEMATICS

ADDITION AND SUBTRACTION OF FRACTIONS, INTEGERS, AND DECIMALS

Many of our mathematical errors are caused by sloppiness. It is critical to have columns lined up neatly and decimal points properly aligned. It is also imperative that one understands the basic vocabulary of math. Examples and explanations of various types of problems on the ATPE test are provided. Work out the sample problems.

Practice Exercises

1. Find the sum of 27, 6278, 341, 9, and 6218

    a. 6,432,   b. 43,276,   c. 285,   d. 12,873

The first thing one must understand is that a sum is the total of all the numbers added. By looking at the answers one could safely guess the correct answer to be *d*, which it is. Looking at the two six thousand numbers, one realizes the answer will be about 12,000. Unfortunately, the test will have an *e* added to their multiple-guess answer selection which will state, "none of the above." This may be the answer so it is best to solve each problem; not guess by estimating.

```
  27
6278
 341
   9
6218
```

Always keep your columns neat, look at the answers before working out the problem, solve the problem as efficiently as possible and continue on to the next problem without rechecking. ATPE is a timed test; work quickly but neatly, and you will save time.

2. What is the difference between 6324 and 467?

    a. 6857,   b. 5867,   c. 5857,   d. 5957

One must understand that difference means the amount by which one number differs from another. Calculators are not allowed during the test, so practice solving these problems quickly and carefully. This time the answer is not as easy to detect at first glance. By subtracting 467 from 6324, one would arrive at the answer *c*.

```
 6324
- 467
-----
 5857
```

Reminder: sum = add   difference = subtract

3. What is the difference between 3.05 and 2.5?

   3.05 - 2.5 equals:

   a. 0.55,   b. 1.55,   c. 1.00,   d. 1.45

The answer is *a*. The problem is read three *and* five-hundredths minus two *and* five-tenths. To be able to read decimal numerals is important. Always line up your decimal points neatly.

```
 3.05
-2.50
  .55
```

The chart below shows that a 5 in the hundreds place has a value of 5 x 100, or 500. A 5 in the hundredths place has a value of 5 x 1/100, or 5/100. Another name for 5/100 is 0.05.

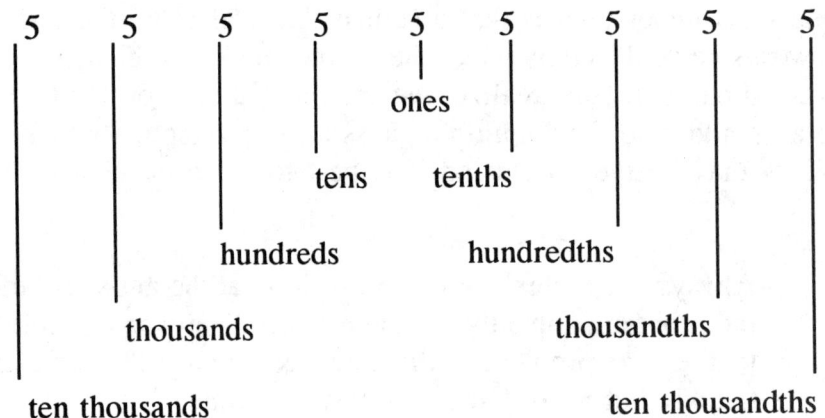

4. 32.06 + 435.2 + 0.51 + 1.67 equals:

   a. 777.6,   b. 7.776,   c. 4.6944,   d. 469.44

```
 32.06
435.20
  0.51
  1.67
------
469.44
```

Place these numerals in columns and you find *d* is the correct answer.

ATPE STUDY GUIDE

5. $\dfrac{11}{12} - \dfrac{7}{9}$ equals:

   a. $\dfrac{4}{3}$,   b. $\dfrac{5}{36}$,   c. $\dfrac{4}{9}$,   d. $\dfrac{15}{21}$

To solve this problem, one must find a common denominator. The numerator is the top number, the denominator is the bottom number. To arrive at the correct answer, *b*, one must understand why 36 is the common denominator.

$$\dfrac{11 \times 3}{12 \times 3} = \dfrac{33}{36}$$

$$\dfrac{7 \times 4}{9 \times 4} = \dfrac{28}{36}$$

$$\dfrac{33}{36} - \dfrac{28}{36} = \dfrac{5}{36}$$

6. Here is another subtraction problem:

$$\dfrac{1}{2} - \dfrac{1}{3} =$$

   a. $\dfrac{2}{5}$,   b. $\dfrac{2}{6}$,   c. $\dfrac{2}{3}$,   d. $\dfrac{1}{6}$

The answer is d. $\dfrac{1}{2} = \dfrac{3}{6}$ 2 x 3 equals 6   1 x 3 equals 3

$\dfrac{1}{3} = \dfrac{2}{6}$ 3 x 2 equals 6   1 x 2 equals 2

Therefore: $\dfrac{3}{6} - \dfrac{2}{6} = \dfrac{1}{6}$

Remember to multiply the denominator and the numerator by the same number.

7. $\frac{1}{2} + \frac{1}{6} = ?$

   a. $\frac{31}{40}$, b. $\frac{8}{12}$, c. $\frac{1}{8}$, d. $\frac{2}{12}$, e. None of these

This is a problem many miss because they choose **None of these**. *B* is the correct answer. The problem doesn't ask for the answer in terms of the least common denominator. 8/12 is the same thing as 4/6 and 2/3. Be careful, these may be tricky problems for you.

Practice with these:

1. 74 − 26.4 equals:

   a. 45.6

   b. 47.6

   c. 57.6

   d. 48.4

   e. None of the above

2. $\frac{2}{5} + \frac{3}{8}$ equals:

   a. $\frac{31}{40}$

   b. $\frac{5}{13}$

   c. $\frac{31}{13}$

   d. $\frac{5}{3}$

   e. None of the above

3. 6.9 − 4.87 equals:

   a. 2.17

   b. 2.13

   c. 2.03

   d. 1.03

   e. None of the above

4. 36 + 3.6 + 243 + 7.14 equals:

   a. 2897.4

   b. 28.974

   c. 2.8974

   d. 28974

   e. None of the above

ATPE STUDY GUIDE

Answers: 1. b, 2. a, 3. c, 4. e

MULTIPLICATION AND DIVISION OF FRACTIONS, DECIMALS, AND INTEGERS

Dividing Fractions and Whole Numbers

With a little review these types of problems will come back to you. Look at this problem: 8 ÷ 1/2 equals. The divisor (½) is inverted so that 8 ÷ 1/2 becomes 8 x 2/1. The division sign is changed to a multiplication sign. The numerators are multiplied. Then the denominators are multiplied. The quotient for 8 ÷ 1/2 is 16.

$$8 \div \frac{1}{2} = 8 \times \frac{2}{1} = \frac{16}{1} = 16 \qquad \frac{8}{1} \times \frac{2}{1} = \frac{16}{1} = 16$$

In the problem $14 \div \frac{2}{5} = ?$, think of the dividend, 14, as $\frac{14}{1}$

The divisor, $\frac{2}{5}$, is inverted so that $14 \div \frac{2}{5}$ becomes $14 \times \frac{5}{2}$

Both 14 and 2 are divided by 2. The numerators are multiplied. Then the denominators are multiplied.

The quotient for $14 \div \frac{2}{5}$ is 35 $\qquad 14 \div \frac{2}{5} = \frac{\cancel{14}^{7}}{1} \times \frac{5}{\cancel{2}_{1}} = \frac{35}{1} = 35$

Examples:

1. $\frac{3}{4} \div 4 =$ 2. $9 \div \frac{3}{5}$ is:

     a. $\frac{4}{16}$ c. $\frac{3}{16}$ a. $\frac{42}{3}$ c. $\frac{27}{5}$

     b. $\frac{1}{4}$ d. $\frac{12}{4}$ b. 15   d. $\frac{3}{45}$

Answers:

1. c, 2. b   (note: $\frac{45}{3}$ is 15)

Dividing Fractions and Mixed Numbers

Study the work that is shown below. The mixed numbers are changed to improper fractions. Next the divisor is inverted. Before the numerators and the denominators are multiplied, cancellation is done. Then the answer is written in lowest terms.

$$2\frac{5}{6} \div 1\frac{8}{9} = \frac{17}{6} \div \frac{17}{9} = \frac{\cancel{17}^{1}}{\cancel{6}_{2}} \times \frac{\cancel{9}^{3}}{\cancel{17}_{1}} = \frac{3}{2} = 1\frac{1}{2}$$

To check the work, think this way:

$$1\frac{1}{2} \times 1\frac{8}{9} \text{ should equal } 2\frac{5}{6}$$

$$1\frac{8}{9} \times 1\frac{1}{2} = \frac{17}{\cancel{9}_{3}} \times \frac{\cancel{3}^{1}}{2} = \frac{17}{6} = 2\frac{5}{6}$$

$$1\frac{8}{9} = \frac{17}{9} \quad \text{because} \quad \begin{array}{l}(9 \times 1) + 8 = 17 \\ 9 + 8 = 17\end{array}$$

$$\frac{17}{6} = 2\frac{5}{6} \quad \text{because} \quad 6\overline{)17} \begin{array}{r} 2 \\ \underline{12} \\ 5 \end{array}$$

six goes into 17 two times with $\frac{5}{6}$ left over

Find the quotients:

1. $\dfrac{1}{4} \div \dfrac{4}{5} =$ 2. $\dfrac{2}{3} \div \dfrac{3}{5} =$

    a. $\dfrac{1}{4}$ a. $\dfrac{9}{10}$

    b. $\dfrac{4}{20}$ b. $\dfrac{6}{15}$

    c. $\dfrac{16}{5}$ c. $1\dfrac{1}{9}$

    d. 4 d. $\dfrac{3}{5}$

    e. $\dfrac{5}{16}$ e. $\dfrac{15}{6}$

Answers: 1. e, 2. c ($\dfrac{10}{9}$ is the same as $1\dfrac{1}{9}$)

Placing the decimal point in a product

To multiply fractional numbers, find the product of the numerators and the product of the denominators.

$$\dfrac{1}{10} \times \dfrac{1}{10} = \dfrac{1 \times 1}{10 \times 10} = \dfrac{1}{100}$$

$$\dfrac{1}{10} \times \dfrac{75}{100} = \dfrac{1 \times 75}{10 \times 100} = \dfrac{75}{1000}$$

$$\dfrac{3}{10} \times \dfrac{4}{1} = \dfrac{3 \times 4}{10 \times 1} = \dfrac{12}{10} = 1\dfrac{2}{10}$$

If the numbers are named by decimals, the products will have decimals.

0.1 x 0.1 is 0.01   0.1 x 0.75 is 0.075   0.3 x 4 is 1.2

MATHEMATICS

The correct number of decimal places in a product equals the sum of the numbers of decimal places in the factors.

```
    0.373 -- (3)        1.62 -- (2)         1.42 -- (2)
    x 0.6 -- (1)        x 8  -- (0)         x 0.03 -- (2)

    0.2238 -- (4)       12.96 -- (2)        0.0426 -- (4)
```

Practice Problems:

1.   806
   x 0.908

   a. 731.848
   b. 7318.48
   c. 73.1848
   d. 806.908

2.   3167
   x .004

   a. 126.68
   b. 1.2668
   c. .12668
   d. 12.668

3.   6 x 0.5 is:

   a. 3
   b. 6.5
   c. .30
   d. 30

Answers: 1. a,   2. d,   3. a

Decimals and division:

When a decimal is divided by a whole number, the division is the same as for whole numbers. The number of decimal places in the quotient is the same as the number of decimal places in the dividend.

1. Find 63.9 ÷ 9:

   a. 575. 1,   b. 57.51,   c. 7.1,   d. 71

The answer is c.

```
      7.1
   9 ) 63.9
       63
        9
        9
```

Be neat. Line up the decimal point.

ATPE STUDY GUIDE

2. Find 10 ÷ 8:

    a. 125,   b. .125,   c. 12.5,   d. 1.25

The answer is *d*.

```
       1.25
   8 )10.00
       8
       20
       16
       40
       40
```

If there is no decimal point in the dividend, place one immediately after the last digit in the dividend and annex zeros so that division may be continued to the number of decimal places desired.

Practice:

1. 23)9936

    a. 532
    b. 43.2
    c. 432
    d. 4320

2. 46)1729.6

    a. 37.6
    b. 376
    c. 376.0
    d. 3.76

3. 21,918 ÷ 26 is:

    a. 0.843
    b. 569,868
    c. .0012
    d. 843

Answers: 1. c, 2. a, 3. d

CONVERSION OF FRACTIONS TO PERCENT, DECIMALS TO PERCENT

It is easy to change a common fraction to a decimal fraction if the common fraction is written as tenths, hundredths, thousandths, etc.

$$\frac{1}{10} = .1 \qquad \frac{3}{100} = .03 \qquad \frac{9}{1000} = .009 \qquad \frac{25}{10000} = .0025$$

If a common fraction is not written as tenths, hundredths, etc., divide the numerator by the denominator to change it to a decimal fraction.

What percent represents $\frac{1}{4}$?

    a. 40%,   b. 10%,   c. 25%   d. 50%

MATHEMATICS

The answer is *c*.

```
      .25
   ─────
 4)1.00
    8
   ──
    20
    20
   ──
```

When we put something in percent form, we move the decimal two places to the <u>right</u> and add the percent sign (%). Ratios such as 25 per 100 or 75 per hundred are percents because percent means per hundred. Any ratio can be named as a percent.

$$\frac{1}{4} = \frac{n}{100} \qquad 100 = 4n \quad 25 = n \qquad \text{Therefore:} \quad \frac{1}{4} = \frac{25}{100} = 25 \text{ percent.}$$

To find a percent of a number, you must know how to change a percent to a decimal fraction. To change a percent to a decimal, drop the percent sign (%) and move the decimal point two places to the <u>left.</u>

Examples:

$$12\% = .12 \qquad 10\% = .10 = .1$$

To change a decimal fraction to a percent, move the decimal point two places to the <u>right</u>. Then place the percent sign at the right of the numeral.

$$.7 = .70 = 70\% \qquad .125 = 12.5\% = 12\frac{1}{2}\%$$

Practice:

1. What is the correct form of $\frac{3}{8}$ expressed as a percent?

    a. 0.375%,   b. 37.5%,   c. 38%,   d. $\frac{3}{8}$%

2. What is 2.305 expressed as a percent?

    a. 23.05%,   b. 2.305%,   c. 230.5%,   d. 2305%

3. What is .27 expressed as a percent?

    a. 270%,   b. 27%,   c. 2.7%,   d. .028%

Answers: 1. b,   2. c,   3. b

Let's Review

1. $\dfrac{9}{14} \times \dfrac{1}{3}$ is:

    a. $\dfrac{14}{27}$

    b. $\dfrac{3}{14}$

    c. $\dfrac{41}{42}$

2. 3 x .09 is:

    a. .027

    b. .27

    c. 2.7

3. 27,603 - 4,987 is:

    a. 4,411

    b. 32,590

    c. 22,616

Answers: 1. b (remember $\dfrac{9}{42}$ is the same as $\dfrac{3}{14}$),   2. b,   3. c

UNDERSTANDING BAR/LINE GRAPHS

Interpreting graphs on the ATPE requires care and concentration before selecting an answer. Study the bar and line graphs on the test carefully. Here are a couple of examples:

The graph to the right gives the number of deer observed in a game preserve on five consecutive days. How many more deer were seen on Thursday than Monday?

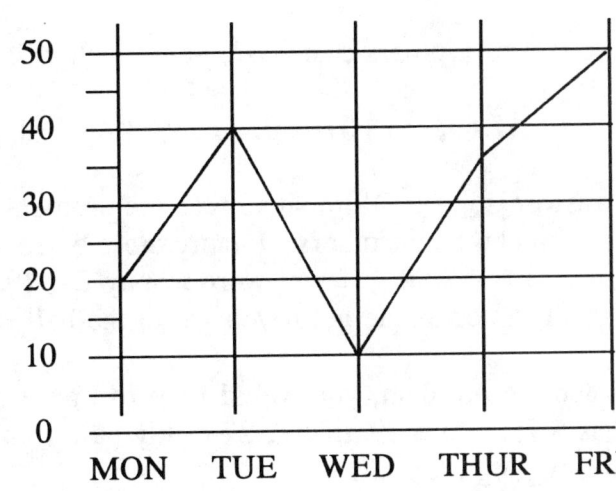

a. 15, b. 40, c. 5, d. 20, e. None of these

MATHEMATICS

The answer is *a*. Monday 20 deer were observed, Thursday 35 deer were observed. The difference is 15.

The graph to the right gives the number of visitors to a museum during four different weeks. If each * represents 20 people, how many visitors were there during week three?

MUSEUM VISITORS	
WEEK 1	* * * * * * * *
WEEK 2	* * * *
WEEK 3	* * * * * * * * * *
WEEK 4	* * * * * * *

a. 29,   b. 7,   c. 21,   d. 140,   e. None of these

The correct answer is *e*. 10 times 20 equals 200. Read the graphs carefully; don't allow them to deceive you.

WORD PROBLEMS

For many, word problems are mind-boggling. If you read the problem carefully, simplifying it as much as possible, you will be able to solve it correctly. Try not to let the problem frustrate you. Think it out in terms with which you are familiar.

Mind-boggling Examples:

1. If 3 candy bars cost $.87, how much will 27 candy bars cost?

    a. $7.83,   b. $78.30,   c. $23.49,   d. $70.47,   e. None of these

The answer is not *e*. Without solving the problem with pencil and paper, does one answer look more correct than the others? Picture those barrels of candy bars near the supermarket cashiers that say: 3 for $.90. If you were to buy 27, (9 times more than 3), the answer would be $8.10. This technique helps you get in the ballpark. The answer is *a*.

To solve the problem, you would have to figure out the cost of one candy bar. $.87 divided by 3 is $.29. At $.29 apiece, 27 candy bars (multiply 27 x $.29) would cost $7.83. Not so mind-boggling after all, is it?

ATPE STUDY GUIDE

2. What would $30 worth of groceries cost if prices rose 8%?

   a. $38.00,   b. $30.08,   c. $33.00,   d. $32.40

The answer is *d*. Think back to what 8% is equivalent to. 8% is the same as .08. $30.00 x .08 is $2.40. If prices rose 8%, that would mean an increase of $2.40, giving us a total of $32.40. In some areas of Arizona we pay a 6% sales tax, meaning we pay 6 cents more for every dollar we spend.

"Approximately" word problems:

1. <u>Approximately</u> how far can a car travel in 6 hrs. if it is traveling at an average speed of 59 m.p.h.?

   a. 10 m.p.h.
   b. 10 mi.
   c. 360 m.p.h.
   d. 360 mi.
   e. None of the above

Once again, a basic vocabulary is necessary. M.p.h. means miles per hour. Mi. means miles. Notice the word *approximately* is underlined. This is not a trick or a typographical error, it's a hint. *Approximately* means round off the numbers.

The question is asking us how far can a car travel. That tells us the answer will be in miles, not miles per hour. If it asked how fast a car can travel, the answer would be in m.p.h.

> To solve this problem, round the 59 to 60 and multiply by 6. 60 x 6 is 360. This is why *d* is correct. Frequently *e* is selected as the answer because people multiply 6 by 59. Be alert for problems that use the words *approximately* and *round off*.

2. It takes John approximately 15 minutes to pick all the fruit off a fruit tree. If there are 23 trees in an orchard, which of the following is the <u>best</u> time for John to begin the job in order to be finished by 5:00 p.m.?

   a. 10:00 a.m.
   b. 11:00 a.m.
   c. 12:00 a.m.
   d. 1:00 p.m.
   e. 2:00 p.m.

Oh, mercy, this one requires us to figure out a few things. Notice the word *approximately* is used but this time it is not underlined. It is still important you recognize the word and round off numbers. The word *best* emphasizes that you are not to say John should begin picking fruit off trees at 6:00 a.m. to make certain he is finished by 5:00 p.m.

The answer is *b*. To solve this conundrum, we must notice it takes 15 minutes to pick the fruit from one tree. Because 23 trees were picked, we must multiply 23 by 15, giving us 345 *MINUTES*, not fruit. Now we need to figure out how many hours and minutes 345 minutes is equal to. With 60 minutes in an hour, how many hours are in 345 minutes?

```
        5
60 ) 345
     300
      45
```

The remainder, 45, is the same as three quarters of an hour. 345 minutes is equivalent to 5 and three-quarter hours.

Since it's an *approximately* problem, round the 5-3/4 hours to six hours. If it will take John about six hours to pick the fruit off the trees, what time must he begin? From 12:00 to 5:00 would be 5 hours. We need six hours, making the starting hour 11:00 a.m. Nothing to it, just take it step-by-step.

Spin Your Wheels and Solve these Mind-Bogglers:

1. During a trip, Mike used 7.9 gallons of gas. *Approximately* how much did he spend for gas on the trip if each gallon costs $1.29?

    a. $10.40,   b. $9.19,   c. $6.61,   d. $1.63,   e. None of these

2. If 1 inch is equal to 0.0254 meters, how many inches are there in 2 meters?

    a. 0.0508,   b. 0.0127,   c. 78.74,   d. 2.0254,   e. None of these

3. The Sock Rack has men's socks for sale at 3 pairs for $2.00. What do 12 pairs cost?

    a. $6.00,   b. $8.00,   c. $7.50,   d. $12.00,   e. None of these

Answers: 1. a,   2. c,   3. b

ATPE STUDY GUIDE

Explanation to the Mind-Bogglers

1. To solve, multiply $1.30 times 8 gallons. Remember, it's an "approximate" problem.

2. Set it up like this: 1 inch equals 0.0254 meters
   ? inches equal 2.0000 meters

$$\frac{1 \text{ inch}}{0.0254 \text{ meters}} = \frac{? \text{ inches}}{2 \text{ meters}} = 2 \div .0254$$

Move the decimal 4 places

```
              78.74
       .0254 ) 2.0000∧
              1 778
              2220
              2032
              1880
              1778
              1020
              1016
                 4
```

3. First you need to find the number of $2.00 units.

```
        4
     3 ) 12
```

Then multiply the number of units by the cost per unit.

4 (units) × $2.00 (cost) = $8.00

AVERAGING

To average means to add two or more numbers and divide the sum by the number of numbers you added. The following examples will make this definition more clear.

1. During 3 home games, Troy scored 14 points, 28 points, and 33 points. What was the average number of points scored per game?

   a. 75 points, b. 25 points, c. 225 points, d. 8 points

The answer is *b*. 14+28+33 is 75. 75 divided by 3 (number of games) is 25.

2. The weights of the four starting defensive linemen for the Tigers are 238.6 lbs., 261.5 lbs., 240.3 lbs., and 227.6 lbs. What is the average weight of the starting line?

   a. 242 lbs.
   b. 968 lbs.
   c. 3872 lbs.
   d. 127.5 lbs.
   e. None of the above

The answer is *a*. Find the sum of all four and divide the total by 4.

Remember to do both steps: find the total, then divide by the number of things you added.

PERIMETER AND AREA

Once you learn the formulas for both, you should be able to solve the problems.

Area of a Square: length x width

Area of a Rectangle: length x width

Perimeter of a Square: side + side + side + side

Perimeter of a Rectangle: side + side + side + side.

Examples:

1. What is the perimeter of a square which is 6 feet on each side?

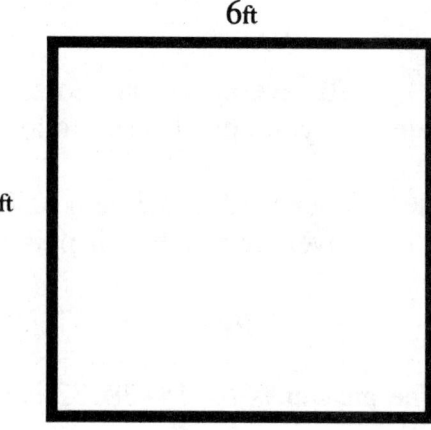

   a. 36 ft.
   b. 36 square feet
   c. 12 ft.
   d. 24 ft.
   e. None of the above

The answer is *d* because 6 + 6 + 6 + 6 is 24.

ATPE STUDY GUIDE

2. What is the perimeter of the rectangle shown ?

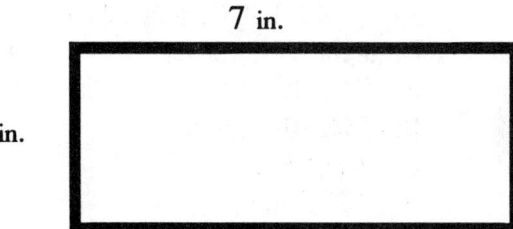

   a. 21 inches
   b. 10 inches
   c. 20 inches
   d. 42 inches
   e. None of the above

The answer is *c*. Remember the difference between area and perimeter. 7 + 7 + 3 + 3.

3. What is the area of the rectangle shown?

   a. 21 square inches
   b. 10 square inches
   c. 20 square inches
   d. 42 square inches
   e. None of the above

The answer is *a*. 7 x 3 is 21.

4. A room is rectangular, 10 ft. wide by 13 ft. long, and a rug 9 ft. by 12 ft. is on the floor. How much of the floor area is *not* covered by the rug?

   a. 1 ft.^{2}
   b. 2 ft.^{2}
   c. 22 ft.^{2}
   d. 108 ft.^{2}
   e. None of the above

The answer is *c*.   Those small 2's are another way of saying square.   22 ft.^{2} = 22 sq. ft.

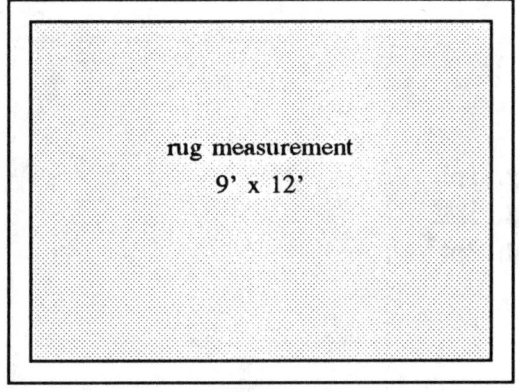

room measurement 10' x 13'

To solve this problem, subtract the number of square feet in the rug from the number of square feet in the room.

> room: 10' x 13' = 130 sq. ft.
>
> rug: 9' x 12' = 108 sq. ft.

MATHEMATICS

Find the area of the room   10 x 13 = 130 sq. ft.

Find the rug's area   9 x 12 = <u>108 sq. ft.</u>

Find the difference   22 sq. ft.

Write the formula for area: _____

Write the formula for perimeter: _____

LIQUID MEASUREMENTS

To solve the liquid-measurement problems you will need to know how many quarts are in a gallon and how many pints are in a quart.

2 pints equal one quart.
4 quarts equal one gallon.

Examples:

1. A container has 3 gal., 2 qt., 1 pt. of liquid. A second container has 5 gal., 3 qt., 1 pt. of the same liquid. What is the sum of the liquid in the two containers?

    a. 15 gal.
    b. 15 quarts
    c. 9 gal. 2 qt.
    d. 8 gal. 7 qt.
    e. None of the above

The answer is c.

Set up the problem like this:
        3gal. 2qt. 1pt.
       <u>+5gal. 3qt. 1pt.</u>
        8gal. 5qt. 2pt.

Remember:

2 pints make one quart.   4 quarts make one gallon.

ATPE STUDY GUIDE

Therefore:

   8 gallons plus 4 of the 5 quarts make 9 gallons, the 2 pints make one quart which added to the remaining one quart totals 2 quarts.

2. What is the sum of: 3 gal. 2 qt. 3 pt.
                        +5 gal. 2 qt. 4 pt.

   a. 9 gal. 1 qt. 1 pt.
   b. 8 gal. 5 qt. 7 pt.
   c. 2 gal. 1 qt.
   d. 10 gal.
   e. None of the above

The answer is **9 gal. 3 qt. 1 pt.** making it *e*.

TIME PROBLEMS

   Time problems are not too difficult, providing you remember there are 60 minutes in an hour and 60 seconds in a minute.

Examples:

1.   4 hrs. 23 min.
       +5 hrs. 51 min.

   a. 10 hrs. 14 min.
   b. 1 hr. 28 min.
   c. 9 hrs. 28 min.
   d. 204 hrs. 115 min.
   e. 8 hrs. 64 min.

The answer is *a*. There are 74 minutes which is converted to 1 hour, 14 minutes.

2. Bob earns $4.50 per hour, and Mary earns $3.70 per hour. If they each work 30 hours, how much more does Bob earn.

   a. $80.00
   b. $8.00
   c. $24.00
   d. $2.40
   e. None of the above

MATHEMATICS

Bob earns $24.00 more than Mary every 30 hours. To figure this problem out, you must multiply each of their salaries by 30 hours and then find the difference. Or faster, compute the difference in their pay per hour as .80 and multiply that by 30 hours to derive the same $24.00 answer.

Practice Exercises:

1. 2 hr. 40 min. 30 sec.
   +3 hr. 20 min. 30 sec.

   a. 5 hr. 70 min. 40 sec.
   b. 6 hr. 50 min. 49 sec.
   c. 6 hr. 1 min.
   d. 6 hr. 10 min.
   e. None of the above

2. Mary went to work at 8:45 a.m. and got off at 4:26 p.m. the same day. How long did she work?

   a. 7 hrs. 19 min.
   b. 7 hrs. 41 min.
   c. 12 hrs. 71 min.
   d. 13 hrs. 11 min.
   e. None of the above

Answers: 1. c, 2. b

If you find problem number two confusing, try thinking of the times as 8:45 and 4:45. Mary would then have put in 8 hours of work. Find the difference between 4:45 and 4:26. 45 minus 26 is 19. Since she worked 19 minutes less than a full 8 hours, subtract 19 minutes from 60 minutes, giving us 41 minutes. It is frequently helpful to round numbers off and then find the difference.

METRIC

There is no reason to experience *metric anxiety* over this portion of the test. There are a few basic formulas that are useful to memorize:

Length

10 millimeters (mm)	=	1 centimeter
10 centimeters (cm)	=	1 decimeter
10 decimeters (dm)	=	1 meter
1000 meters (m)	=	1 kilometer (km)

Weight

1000 milligrams (mg)	=	1 gram
1000 grams (g)	=	1 kilogram
1000 kilograms (kg)	=	1 metric ton (t)

Try this pneumonic to help you remember metric prefixes.

Kiss	**Her**	**Darn**	**You**	**Don't**	**Cry**	**Mom**
Kilo	Hecta	Deka	Unit	Deci	Centi	Mili
1000	100	10		1/10	1/100	1/1000

Examples:

1. 10 mm is the same as:

    a. 1 cm
    b. 1 dm
    c. 100 m
    d. 1,000 m
    e. None of the above

The answer is *a*. Memorize the metric formulas.

2. 1 cm is equal to:

    a. 10 m
    b. 100 m
    c. 1/10 m
    d. 1/100 m
    e. None of the above

The answer is *d*. *Centi* means "hundredth."

3. If 1 km is equal to 1,000 m, how many square meters are in 5 square kilometers?

    a. 5,000
    b. 50,000
    c. 500,000
    d. 5,000,000
    e. None of the above

The answer is *d*. Whenever you square something, you multiply the number to be squared by itself. 1,000 x 1,000 equals 1,000,000. The 5 is already in terms of square, so you multiply 1,000,000 x 5 to get the answer 5,000,000 square kilometers.

Practice

1. 1,000 kilograms are equal to _____ metric ton(s).

2. 10 cm are equal to _____ decimeter.

3. 10 millimeters are equal to _____ centimeter.

4. 1,000 grams are equal to _____ kilogram.

Answers: 1. 1,   2. 1,   3. 1,   4. 1

GRAMMAR

PERIODS, QUESTION MARKS AND EXCLAMATION MARKS

All of us are familiar with periods, question marks, and exclamation marks. The questions on the test regarding this area are frequently missed because we are so familiar with these punctuation marks that we overlook their absence or misuse. In order to do well, we must read the questions carefully and listen to the tone of the author's statement.

A period represents a *declarative* type of sentence. A declarative sentence simply states a fact: "I went to the dentist yesterday." Question marks represent *interrogative* sentences. As the name implies, interrogative sentences ask direct questions: "When did you last visit a dentist?" *Exclamatory* sentences express enthusiasm, surprise, and commands: "Oh, no! I forgot to brush my teeth before my dentist appointment!" The way you punctuate a sentence affects the meaning of your sentence. For example:

(a) Your cat ran to the store.

(b) Your cat ran to the store?

(c) Your cat ran to the store!

Without any additional information supplied with these statements, it is difficult to understand the writer's intentions. Providing you were asked to punctuate the above statements without any supporting evidence to the content, any punctuation mark could be correct. Usually on the ATPE test, there are short passages to punctuate. For practice, punctuate the following passage:

"I've never been in Egypt (1) Indeed I have (2) That's the one thing you can be sure of (3) I have been all over the world and seen many things stranger than people walking backward (4) I wonder what you would have said if I had come along walking on my hands the way they do in Farthest India (5) "

This is a passage from the children's book, Pippi Longstocking.

Number one is a question and the rest are periods. Number two could have also been read as an exclamatory statement.

This time, punctuate the passage and add quotation marks.

Annika said anxiously, Do you live here all alone

Of course not said Pippi. Mr. Nilsson and the horse live here too

Answers:

Annika said anxiously, "Do you live here all alone?"

"Of course not!" said Pippi. "Mr. Nilsson and the horse live here too."

Self-Test

Supply the necessary punctuation for the following passage. Be careful to place your punctuation marks inside the quotation marks when necessary.

She had flown past, attracted by the deep groans the mother uttered in her labor _(1)_ The magpie perched on a neighboring branch. _(2)_ What a beautiful child _(3)_ she kept repeating _(4)_ Receiving no answer, she went on talkatively, _(5)_ How amazing to think that he should be able to get right up and walk _(6)_ How interesting _(7)_ I've never seen the like of it before in all my days _(8)_ Of course, I'm still young, only a year out of the nest, you might say. But I think it's wonderful. A child like that, hardly a minute in this world, and beginning to walk already _(9)_ I call that remarkable _(10)_ Really, I find that everything you dare do is remarkable. Can he run, too _(11)_

This is quoted from the tender story, <u>Bambi.</u>

Answers: 1. (.), 2. ("), 3. (,"), 4. (.), 5. ("), 6. (!),

7. (!), 8. (.), 9. (!), 10. (.), 11. (?")

COMMA FOR CLARITY

The comma is the most difficult punctuation mark to master because of its wide variety of uses. Knowing the comma is such a versatile tool that we tend to overuse it. You must remember that commas do have a purpose. More than any other punctuation mark, the comma guides the reader, organizes groups of words into meaningful units, and makes it easier for a writer to transmit the intended meaning accurately.

Uses of Commas

Use a comma before the conjunction in a compound sentence.

> Of course Tommy and Annika asked to go too, and their kind father immediately gave them some money.

Conjunctions are the words used to connect phrases, clauses, or words. These words are conjunctions: and, but, or, nor, for, and yet.

A compound sentence has two independent clauses. A clause is a group of words that, by itself, might be a sentence.

If the two clauses are very short and closely related, the comma may be omitted.

> Pippi could sing but she couldn't carry a tune.

<u>Adverbial clauses</u> are not independent. They tell the how, when, why, where, or how much of what happens in the main clause that follows.

> After the heat of the day, the evening came as a welcome relief to all.

Commas are usually used to set off <u>introductory elements</u> which are not part of an independent clause. Prepositional phrases, participial phrases, and adverbial clauses are the most common introductory elements.

> In the first place, I love mushrooms.

Prepositional phrases contain at least a preposition and an object of the preposition. They are usually set off by a comma when they are before a clause.

COMMON PREPOSITIONS

about	beyond	past
above	but	round
across	by	since
after	down	through
against	during	till
along	ere	to
amid	except	toward
among	for	under
around	from	underneath
at	in	until
before	into	unto
behind	like	up
below	of	upon
beneath	off	with
beside	on	within
between	over	without

<u>Participial phrases</u> contain a word that acts like both a verb and an adjective.

    The boy, frightened by the noise, called for help.

<u>Transitional phrases</u>, which connect our sentences together, tend to use commas. Words like: *nevertheless, therefore, however* are frequently used to show the relationship between two sentences.

    Petunia flirted with Pudge whenever she could. Nevertheless, Pudge liked her.

Use a comma to separate three or more items in a <u>series.</u> When used this way, a comma is always placed before the word *and* in order to keep the meaning clear.

    Candy bars, cracker jacks, and cotton candy are favorite treats for many children today.

Use commas to set off *nonrestrictive* elements in a sentence. *Restrictive* modifiers are those necessary to limit the meaning of the word modified; the sentence would mean something else if the restrictive modifier was taken out.

    We shall agree to the proposal if you accept our conditions.

    Nonrestrictive elements contribute additional information but are not necessary for getting the meaning of the sentence across.

ATPE STUDY GUIDE

We voted for the proposal, although we were against it.

Use commas to set off the name of someone spoken to directly, or to set off words of direct address used in place of a name.

Imelda, let us see your pretty smile.

Ladies and Gentlemen, I have an interesting tale to tell you.

Use commas to set off all items after the first in dates and addresses:

My address is 3001 Zany Lane, Serendipity, Arizona 85001.

Note that the ZIP code is not set off by a comma.

My date of birth is December 29, 1962.

Use commas to insure clarity.

Outside, the air was much cooler. (It would be more confusing if it said: "Outside the air was much cooler.")

Use commas to set off *yes*, *no*, and interjections:

Well, maybe I will go.
No, I won't go.

Use commas to separate adjectives of equal value:

We were hit by a dreary, tedious, chilly monsoon this summer.

Do not put a comma between the last coordinate adjective and the word these adjectives modify. You will have to remember how this rule differs from the series rule.

Use commas to identify *appositives* in a sentence. An appositive is a noun or group of words used like a noun that gives another name to a noun in the sentence.

Pippi Longstocking, the strongest girl in the world, could carry her horse above her head for miles.

Use commas to set off contrasted elements with *not*:

Those are spaghetti noodles, not worms, on your plate.

GRAMMAR

Use commas to set off degrees and titles from names:

Monroe Meathead, Jr., entitled himself Monroe Meathead, Esq., out of smugness.

As you can see, commas are versatile and are used with a purpose. Practice working out the following exercises. Try to think each sentence out for the meaning intended by the writer.

Self-Test

Supply the necessary punctuation for the following:

1. "Of course " replied the mother softly. "But you must pardon me if I don't talk with you now I have so much to do and I still feel a little faint "

2. "Pardon " replied the mother   "I wasn't listening."

3. The little fawn understood not one of the many songs and calls not a word of the conversations.

4. While he suckled the mother continued to caress her little one

5. Every little while she raised her head and listening snuffed the wind

Answers:

1. "Of course," replied the mother softly. "But you must pardon me if I don't talk with you now. I have so much to do, and I still feel a little faint."

2. "Pardon," replied the mother, "I wasn't listening."

3. The little fawn understood not one of the many songs and calls, not a word of the conversations.

4. While he suckled, the mother continued to caress her little one.

5. Every little while she raised her head and, listening, snuffed the wind.

    These, too, are quotes from *Bambi* by Felix Salten.

UNDERLINING TITLES

Titles of books, long poems, dramas, motion pictures, magazines and newspapers, art, the names of ships, and foreign words and phrases should be italicized in print. If italic is not available, such as when writing on the board in your classroom or using most typewriters, underlines must be used.

Examples:

Paradise Lost is an extremely long poem.

Most people have heard of the airship *Hindenburg*.

Lafacadio is a very cynical book.

The *Washington Monthly* is an informative liberal magazine.

There's nothing I enjoy more in the morning than reading *The Arizona Republic* before leaving for work.

Hos ego versiculos feci: tulit alter honores is a Latin phrase many writers use that means, "I wrote these lines; another got the credit for them."

The Glass Menagerie is a popular play.

Gone With The Wind is a classic motion picture.

Recognizing titles of books, names of ships, magazines and newspapers, and poems of great length can be a problem. The more time a person spends reading, the more informed a person will become on these issues. It would be impossible to list all the titles, foreign phrases, names of ships, and whatever else requires underline or italic, if available. The best thing to do is read the ATPE question sensibly, trying to recall if you may have heard a word or phrase in reference to a title or name of a ship.

In addition, underline or italic is sometimes used to emphasize an important phrase or point.

REMEMBER, READING IS AN ESSENTIAL TOOL IN LEARNING!

Self-Test

Correct the following sentences.

1. Why do so many people love the tedious Gone with the Wind?

2. Thinking of the Titanic makes me nervous about my cruise.

3. Do you subscribe to The Arizona Republic?

4. Tonight I am going to see The Glass Menagerie at Coconino High School.

5. Isn't Paradise Lost an extremely long poem?

Answers:

1. Why do so many people love the tedious <u>Gone with the Wind</u>?

2. Thinking of the <u>Titanic</u> makes me nervous about my cruise.

3. Do you subscribe to <u>The Arizona Republic</u>?

4. Tonight I am going to see <u>The Glass Menagerie</u> at Coconino High School.

5. Isn't <u>Paradise Lost</u> an extremely long poem?

HYPHEN

Hyphens are frequently overlooked and considered to be insignificant, but they have an important function. When writing numbers, use a hyphen in the two-word numbers from twenty-one to ninety-nine:

> Back in the olden days, I was able to buy a good car for one hundred seventy-five dollars.

Numbers like *ten thousand*, *three hundred*, and *one million* do not require a hyphen:

> Ten thousand people attended the Nitty Gritty Dirt Band Concert.

Use hyphens to separate the parts of written-out fractions:

> one-fourth, two and one-half, three and three-quarters

Hyphens are necessary to separate a prefix ending in a vowel from a word starting with the same vowel:

fire-eating, re-elect, re-examine

Words, such as: *father-in-law, son-in-law, brother-in-law, mother-in-law, daughter-in-law, sister-in-law; great-grandmother, great-grandfather*, require hyphens.

The hyphen is used after *ex* when it means formerly (e.g., ex-wife).

The hyphen is used after a prefix when followed by a formal noun (e.g., pro-Kennedy).

Use a hyphen in compound words normally spelled with a hyphen and in compound adjectives:

Sue's sister-in-law was a quick-moving lady.

Usually, the hyphen is used to join two words that form a compound adjective that comes before the noun. When the adjective is preceded by an adverb, no hyphen is used:

The quickly moving lady was Sue's sister-in-law.

Hyphens are used to divide a word at the end of a line:

Desert Survival Handbook provides the information necessary to deal with emergencies in the desert.

Some basic rules:

1. A single-syllable word may never be divided.

2. Two letters that make a single sound may not be separated (examples: *th* as in either, *sh* as in smashing, *ai* as in brainpower, *ck* as in luckily).

3. Divide the word after the prefix or before the suffix, unless this alters the pronunciation (examples: pre-natal, anti-disestablishment, dis-place, dis-regard, displace-ment, disregard-ing).

4. Divide the word after a vowel; again, you may not alter the pronunciation (examples: intensi-fied, ana-lyze, inde-cent).

5. Do not divide off fewer than three letters at the end of a line.

The best way to keep up with the proper usage of a word is by using an up-to-date dictionary.

Self-Test

Punctuate the following:

1. semiliterate
2. fireeating
3. exhusband
4. a well known woman
5. proKennedy
6. seventyfour and twofourths
7. scrolllike
8. semiprofessional

Answers:

1. semi-literate
2. fire-eating
3. ex-husband
4. a well-known woman
5. pro-Kennedy
6. seventy-four and two-fourths
7. scroll-like
8. semi-professional

Which of the following words may be divided at the end of a line?

1. through
2. thorough
3. common
4. compound
5. and
6. obey
7. plowed
8. malignant
9. erupt
10. happy
11. drain

Answers:

1. no
2. yes
3. yes
4. yes
5. no
6. no
7. no
8. yes
9. no
10. no
11. no

APOSTROPHE-POSSESSION

Apostrophes are used to show possession. The tricky part is to figure out if it is *'s*, or *s'*.

A name that means more than one is a plural name. When a plural name ends in *s*, only an apostrophe (') is added to make it show possession or relationship.

Examples: boys' hats
girls' shoes

When a plural name does not end in *s*, an *'s* is added to it to make it show possession.

Examples: men's handkerchiefs
women's magazines
children's books

Singular names mean you are talking about one person or animal. An *'s* is added to each name to make it show possession.

Examples: The girl's book (books)
Gloria's pen (pens)
The woodchuck's tail

Summary of Rules:

1. Add an apostrophe plus an *s* to words not ending in *s*: men's, Sam's, people's, ship's.

2. If the word is singular and ends in *s*, add an apostrophe s, unless this makes the word difficult to say: jackass's stubbornness; harness's strength; grass's greenness.

3. If the word is plural and ends in *s* add only the apostrophe: horses' stables, ships' berths, girls' locker room.

Possessive compounds add an *'s* to the last word.

Examples: great-grandfather's car
both mothers-in-law's motorcycles
no one else's business

Joint possession also involves an *'s* to the last word. In cases of individual possession, each word naturally is possessive–this keeps the meaning clear.

Examples:

>Zelda, Frieda, and Harriet's act (joint)
>Zelda's, Frieda's, and Harriet's men were beauties (individuals)

Practice:

Convert the parenthetical material into a possessive plus noun. For example:

>The (blankets belonging to the children) were lovely.
>The children's blankets were lovely.

1. One (hat of a lady) was new, but the other (hats of ladies) were not.

2. (hats for men) were on sale.

3. (governors of twenty states) attended the conference.

Supply the possessive signals necessary for the following in making the parenthetical word or words possessive.

4. (Paul and Pete) brother

5. (someone else) horse

6. (brother-in-law) (ex-wife) alimony

Answers:

1. One lady's hat was new, but the other ladies' hats were not.

2. Men's hats were on sale.

3. Twenty states' governors attended the conference.

4. Paul and Pete's brother.

5. someone else's horse

6. brother-in-law's ex-wife's alimony.

QUOTATION MARKS

Quotation marks are used to signal the exact words of a speaker.

"Well," Scott muttered, "I made a mistake."
She said, "The grass is green."
"I am hungry," Martha whined.

Take notice of the punctuation marks inside the quotation marks.

Quotation marks are to be used with *direct quotations*, not indirect quotations. A direct quotation is the exact words someone said while an indirect quotation expresses the idea of what someone said.

My mother told me I always talked too fast. (indirect)
"You always talk too fast," said Mother. (direct)

Quotation marks are used with the titles of poems, short stories, articles, chapters in books, essays, and songs.

Ike and Tina Turner could get the audience hopping when they sang "Proud Mary."

What may become confusing here is recognizing the differences between titles of books and short stories, long poems and short poems, and titles of movies from songs. Where the one requires italics, the other requires quotation marks.

In *Heidi*, my favorite chapter is "Homesickness."

Self-Test

Punctuate the following sentences:

1. The sky is gray he said, and the sun is hiding behind those clouds.

2. Did he say The sky is blue

3. He asked if it was raining.

4. One of the poems in the book is Lewis Carroll's Jabberwocky.

5. That poem added several words to the English language, among them being slithy, mimsy, and borogroves.

Answers:

1. "The sky is gray," he said, "and the sun is hiding behind those clouds."

2. Did he say, "The sky is blue?"

3. No punctuation needed.

4. One of the poems in the book is Lewis Carroll's "Jabberwocky."

5. That poem added several words to the English language, among them being "slithy," "mimsy," and "borogroves."

COLON

The colon (:) tends to be underused because its purpose isn't understood. When you are providing a list, an explanation, or an example, the colon is used. But do not use a colon immediately after a verb or after "such as." Colons must be preceded by independent clauses.

Formal List:

Due to heavy rains, the following trails at the Grand Canyon have been closed: the Kaibab Trail, the Bright Angel Trail, and the Clear Creek Trail.

Explanation:

Mary provided her boss with the following excuses for always being late to work: flat tire, alarm didn't go off, and she thought it was Saturday.

Example:

Quotation marks are used to enclose those parts of a sentence which are direct quotations: "Great Scott, I thought you forgot about me," Marsha sighed with relief.

Colons are also used to introduce a formal quotation:

Susan Stupendous, speaking from the Senate floor, screamed these words: "I come to bury Caesar, not to praise him."

Use the colon between chapter and verse in books of the Bible (John 3:16); between the act and scene of a play (Hamlet I:3); to separate hour and minute in time designations (7:35 p.m.); after the salutation in a business letter (Dear Editor:); and after headings in the text of books and magazines ("Introduction: The Weaknesses in Public Schools").

Supply punctuation for the following review sentences:

1. The San Diego Zoo's collection of baby animals includes three fascinating little creatures playing together in the same enclosure a baby orangutan a baby chimpanzee and a baby gorilla.

2. Mark Anthony speaking from the Senate floor uttered these words I come to bury Caesar, not to praise him.

3. Three of his faults troubled her most his untidiness his sloppy eating habits and his constantly telling unpleasant truths.

Answers:

1. The San Diego Zoo's collection of baby animals includes three fascinating little creatures playing together in the same enclosure: a baby orangutan, a baby chimpanzee, and a baby gorilla.

2. Mark Antony, speaking from the Senate floor, uttered these words: "I come to bury Caesar, not to praise him."

3. Three of his faults troubled her most: his untidiness, his sloppy eating habits, and his constantly telling unpleasant truths.

SEMICOLONS

The semicolon (;) can be an exasperating punctuation mark. Its purpose is to join two independent clauses when no conjunction (*and, but, for, or, nor, yet*) is used. In general, it is wiser to use a period, but if the two independent clauses are closely associated, a semicolon may be used.

Selecting a dessert from the menu is a difficult procedure; all the selections are delicious.

But it could also be written:

Selecting a dessert from the menu is a difficult procedure. All the selections are delicious.

Or:

Selecting a dessert from the menu is a difficult procedure, for all the selections are delicious.

Sometimes it is difficult to know which route to go. It is important to familiarize yourself with the functions of all the punctuation marks. Usually one choice will appear to be better than the others, yet there will always be those that will cause the linguists to debate.

If several commas are included in both independent clauses of a compound sentence, the semicolon may replace the comma that ordinarily precedes the conjunction between the two clauses.

> The Alm-Uncle was sorry, too, for he had become much attached to the good doctor; and as for Heidi, she did not know what she would do without her dear old friend.

The semicolon is also used between items in a series when the items contain commas:

> I was expected to sweep up, put the stock back, and check the inventory special; prepare the sign for the next day's special; and wait on customers, all the time.

The semicolons were used here because when commas are needed within the items in a series it would be confusing to use more commas to separate the items from each other.

The main thing to watch for is when it would be better to use a period instead of a semicolon, and a semicolon instead of a comma. The semicolon does have definite functions.

Self-Test

Supply the necessary punctuation for the following sentences:

1. She wanted to talk only with Bertha no one else would do.

2. Wilbur's food is your food therefore Wilbur's destiny and your destiny are closely linked.

3. She drove to Holland, Michigan Tuba City, Arizona Telluride, Colorado and Concrete, Washington.

Answers:

1. She wanted to talk only with Bertha; no one else would do.

2. Wilbur's food is your food; therefore, Wilbur's destiny and your destiny are closely linked.

3. She drove to Holland, Michigan; Tuba City, Arizona; Telluride, Colorado; and Concrete, Washington.

USE OF CAPITAL LETTERS

Capital letters are employed to give emphasis to particular words, namely proper nouns and proper adjectives. The difficulty in this principle lies in determining when a noun or adjective is proper, and when a noun or adjective is common. It would be difficult, if not impossible, to list here an exhaustive set of rules to cover every instance. The following rules, however, will be found helpful insofar as they apply to problems in capitalization met daily.

1. Capitalize the first word (a) of a sentence, (b) of a direct quotation, (c) of a line of poetry, or (d) of a formally introduced series of items or phrases following a colon. The first word of a fragmentary quotation is not capitalized.

    He thought the play "was good, but amateurish."
    Turning quickly she said, "Please go now."

    The first word following a colon is *not* capitalized if it is expanding, qualifying, or clarifying what is preceding the colon.

    Intelligence cannot be acquired or increased: it is native.

    The analysis revealed the following: Carbon, six parts; hydrogen, twelve parts; oxygen, six parts.

2. Capitalize the interjection O, but none of the other interjections.

    O powerful western fallen star!   O shades of night—O moody, tearful night!

3. Capitalize all proper nouns.

    Bohemia, China, America, Louis Pasteur, Adam

4. Words derived from proper nouns, and retaining a proper meaning are capitalized.

    Bohemian (of Bohemia)   Venetian (of Venice)

    Do not capitalize words derived from proper nouns for which a common or specialized meaning has been developed.

    china (dishes)   venetian blinds
    pasteurize   plaster of paris

GRAMMAR

5. The following are never capitalized:

aqueduct	ditch	lock	tunnel
breakwater	dry dock	pier	watershed
buoy	floodway	slip	weir
dike	levee	spillway	wharf

The following are capitalized when they follow a proper name:

Archipelago	Desert	Highway	Narrows
Bay	Falls	Hill	Peninsula
Bayou	Forest	Hook	Plateau
Borough	Fork (stream)	Inlet	River
Canal	Fort	Island	Sea
Canyon	Gap	Isle	Sound
Cape	Glacier	Lake	Spring
Channel	Gulch	Mount	Valley
County	Gulf	Mountain	Woods
Creek	Harbor		

6. Capitalize *d', da, della, van, von* when not preceded by a title or forename.

    De Maupassant, but Guy de Maupassant
    Van Gogh, but Vincent van Gogh

    In American and British names these particles are usually capitalized without regard to the above rule, but individual usage should be followed.

    William De Morgan
    Lucretia Van Zandt

7. Capitalize the names of organized bodies and their members to distinguish them from the common meaning.

    Republican Party, a Republican: but a republican (one who believes in a republican form of government.)

    an Elk, but an elk (Elk the club member, but elk the animal.)

8. Capitalize territory, state, nation, union, empire, etc., only when these words refer to a particular political division.

the United States: the Republic, the Nation, the Union;
but a republic, a nation, a union.

Maricopa County: the County; but a county.

9. Capitalize descriptive terms used to designate a definite geographical region or feature.

   the Middle Atlantic States
   the North Pole, the South Pole
   the Western Hemisphere

10. Capitalize names of months and days of the year.

11. Capitalize names of historic events and eras, holidays, and ecclesiastical feast days.

12. Capitalize personification in figures in speech.

    For Nature is neither kind nor cruel, merciless nor merciful; she follows inexorably her immutable laws.

    The Chair introduced the guest speaker.

13. Capitalize all nouns and adjectives denoting the Deity.

    the Holy Ghost   Jehovah
    the Lord   Son of Man

14. Capitalize all names of creeds, religious bodies and their adherents.

    Christian   Buddhist
    Methodist Church   Mohammedan

15. Capitalize all names for the Bible, books of the Bible, and all other sacred books.

    Holy Writ   the Koran
    Scriptures   Exodus

Do not capitalize adjectives derived from such nouns.

    apocryphal   scriptural
    koranic   biblical

GRAMMAR

16. Capitalize all titles preceding a name.

        Doctor Smith   King George
        Professor Gibbs   President Bush
        General Butler   Justice Roberts

Capitalize a title in the second or third person.

        Your Honor   Mr. President
        His Excellency   His Holiness

17. Capitalize the first word and every important word in the title of a book, poem, play, article, essay, work of art, piece of music, report, publication, legal case, and historic document.

        The Dawn of Civilization (book)   Old Lamps of New (essay)
                Death and Transfiguration (music)

Practice:

Which of these words should also be capitalized in the following sentences?

1. I am writing to inquire about a position at Oak tree Camp and to explain my qualifications for working on the staff.

    a. position
    b. tree
    c. staff
    d. None of the above

2. I am a junior varsity cheerleader at Reedville High School in Reedville, Arizona.

    a. junior
    b. varsity
    c. cheerleader
    d. None of the above

3. I learned about the old west from reading novels.

    a. old
    b. novels
    c. west
    d. old and west

ATPE STUDY GUIDE

4. Tonight I am going to hear the president of the United States.

   a. president
   b. of
   c. the
   d. None of the above

5. On my eightieth birthday I received a monkey from uncle Harold.

   a. birthday
   b. uncle
   c. monkey
   d. None of the above

6. We went to a restaurant that specialized in chinese food.

   a. restaurant
   b. food
   c. chinese
   d. None of the above

Answers:

1. b, 2. d, 3. d, 4. a, 5. b, 6. c

SUBJECT-VERB AGREEMENT

With this portion of the test, it is imperative that you recognize the subject and verb. The subject is what is being talked about, and the verb is what it is doing.

   My mother, along with her sisters, shops twice a week.

In this example, *mother* is the subject and *shops* is the verb. "Along with her sisters" is the modifying phrase, which has no effect on the verb.

Underline the subject and verb in the following sentence:

   A stack of letters was on the desk.

The subject is *stack*. *Of letters* is a phrase modifying the subject *stack*. *Was* is the verb.

It is important to understand why a subject is singular or plural so you will use the correct verb. In general, if your subject consists of a group of things, it is normally plural unless you intentionally mean to consider the group as a whole.

> Books and records are what I like best.

The two separate hobbies are equivalent to the word *they*.

> They are what I like best.

When some form of the verb *to be* joins two nouns, the first noun is considered the subject, and the verb agrees with it.

> My favorite fruit is cherries.
> Cherries are my favorite fruit.

Notice how the verb agrees with whichever subject comes first.

There are times when the subject can be singular or plural:

> Ham and eggs is my favorite meal.
> My snake and mouse are friends.

When "or" or "nor" are used to join the subject elements, the verb agrees with the element nearest it.

> Neither Ms. Walsh nor the directors have accepted the offer.

One, each, either, another, none, neither, someone, somebody, and everyone are singular.

> Somebody always talks at the wrong time.
> (He talks at the wrong time.)
> Everyone in the store was provided with a gift.
> (He was provided with a gift.)

Substitute a singular subject (he, she, it) for the troublesome indefinite pronouns.

Collective nouns may be singular or plural depending on whether you think of a group (singular) or separate individuals (plural).

> The team is determined to win. (a group)
> The team come from different parts of the state. (individuals)

The word "there" may be confusing in some sentences:

>There (is, are) the two strangers I mentioned before.

Reverse the sentence to figure out the correct verb:

>The two strangers I mentioned before (is, are) there.

Since there are two strangers, we know it's a plural subject and we can substitute "they are" for the subject.

>They are here.
>There are the two strangers I mentioned before.

Frequently, the subject will appear at the end of a sentence:

1. In my locker (is, are) the bundles of magazines.

Reverse it:

>The *bundles* of magazines *are* in my locker.

2. How long (have, has) the two of them been dating?

Reverse it:

>*They have* been dating how long?

Mentally crossing-out and reversing are two techniques that will assist you a great deal in future use. Let's review:

1. The owner, as well as five of his customers, (was, were) arrested on charges of fraud.

2. The owner, ------------------, (was, were) arrested on charges of fraud.

3. Either the blue pants or the green skirt (look, looks) terrific on you.

4. The green skirt, -------------, (look, looks) terrific on you.

Answers: 1. was, 2. was, 3. looks, 4. looks

And then there are sentences like this:

> This is one of those Cabbage Patch dolls that (crowd, crowds) the shelves at Christmas time.

Even though one Cabbage Patch doll has been selected as a sample, all of the dolls are being discussed.

> They (crowd, crowds) the shelves at Christmas time.

Breaking it down like this simplifies it more, enabling you to find the correct answer.

> This is one of those Cabbage Patch dolls that crowd shelves at Christmas time.

What do you do with a sentence like this?:

> Half of the pie (has, have) been eaten.

Since there is less than one pie in the example, exchange "half of the pie" with a singular subject. (It has been eaten.)

> Half of the pies (has, have) been eaten.

When there are more than one, use a plural subject. (They have been eaten.)

> Two-thirds of the pies (was, were) purchased at the No-Sugar Bakery.

Since there are more than one in the subject, use *they*.

> They were purchased ....

Antecedents are words or statements to which a pronoun refers. This means that if you are talking about *a man*, you cannot refer to him as *they*.

> In this world, everyone gets the life <u>they deserve</u>.

Test it:

> In this world, one gets the life they deserve.

One is singular, and *they* doesn't follow the pattern.

> In this world, *everyone* gets what *he deserves*.

If the antecedent is singular, then the pronoun is singular and takes a singular verb; if the antecedent is plural, then the pronoun is plural and takes a plural verb. The antecedent of a relative pronoun (who, which, or that) is the preceding word or statement to which the pronoun refers:

This is one of the most ineffective birth control methods that have ever been developed.

The antecedent of *that* is *methods*, not *one*. Therefore, *that* is plural and should be followed by a plural verb. To check your work, use the reversal techniques:

Of the birth control methods that have ever been developed, this is one of the most ineffective.

Remember indefinite pronouns (one, either, each, any, anyone, etc.) are singular and take singular verbs:

Each may do as *she pleases*.

Collective nouns (jury, class, committee, team) need to be consistent throughout:

My university was one of the top twenty schools in the nation that was rated for its academic excellence.

Self-Test

1. The watch and the strap (is, are) made of gold.

2. There (is, are) the umbrella and sandwich I must take along.

3. Each of the dogs (is, are) a former winner of the "Nuisance Award."

4. Two-thirds of the shipment (has, have) been confiscated.

Answers:

1. The watch and the strap are made of gold.

2. There are the umbrella and sandwich I must take along.

3. Each of the dogs is a former winner of the "Nuisance Award."

4. Two-thirds of the shipment has been confiscated.

VERB TENSE

The past tense of regular verbs are formed by adding *d* or *ed* to the basic form: skate/skated.

Irregular verbs—those which are not formed by simply adding *d* or *ed*—are more confusing and need to be memorized.

You will need to learn the present tense form (swim), the simple past tense form (swam), and the past participle (have swum). The past participle tense is formed with the verbs *have* and *to be*.

The following list includes those irregular verbs which most frequently give trouble. Go over the list to familiarize yourself with the verbs you feel weakest with. Practice using those which trouble you in your daily speech.

Present	Past	Past Participle
arise	arose	arisen
begin	began	begun
bend	bent	bent
break	broke	broken
build	built	built
burst	burst	burst
choose	chose	chosen
come	came	come
cut	cut	cut
do	did	done
drink	drank	drunk
eat	ate	eaten
fall	fell	fallen
fly	flew	flown
freeze	froze	frozen
get	got	gotten
give	gave	given
go	went	gone
grow	grew	grown
know	knew	known
lay	laid	laid
lead	led	led
run	ran	run
see	saw	seen
speak	spoke	spoken
steal	stole	stolen

swim	swam	swum
take	took	taken
throw	threw	thrown
write	wrote	written

A useful approach in memorizing these forms is to use them in a series of sentences:

Today I swim. Yesterday I swam. Several times I have swum.

The verb *lie* and *lay* are troublesome because the past tense form of *lie*, an irregular verb, is spelled the same as the present tense form of *lay*, a regular verb.

lie	lay	lain
lay	laid	laid

Lie is an intransitive verb meaning to recline; it does not take a direct object.

    I *lie* in the sun everyday.
    Yesterday I *lay* in the sun for twenty minutes.
    I *have lain* in the sun nearly every day this month.

Lay is a transitive verb meaning to put or place; it does take a direct object.

    Sometimes I *lay* my clothes out in the morning.
    Yesterday I *laid* them out.
    I *have laid* them out every day this month.

Lie can also be a regular verb meaning to tell an untruth: lie, lied, lied.

    Sometimes I *lie*.
    Yesterday I *lied*.
    I have lied before.

Another pair of verbs that are frequently confused are *sit* and *set*.

Sit is an intransitive verb meaning to get into a sitting position; it does not take a direct object. *Sit* and *lie* are similar and can be used in the same ways:

    I *sit* in the sun.   I *lie* in the sun.
    Yesterday I *sat* in the sun.   Yesterday I *lay* in the sun.

    I have *sat* in the sun every day this week.
    I have *lain* in the sun every day this week.

Set is a transitive verb meaning to put or place; just like *lay*, it does take a direct object:

> Today I *set* the table. Today I *lay* carpet.
> Yesterday I *set* the table. Yesterday I *laid* the carpet.
>
> Several times I *have set* the table.
> Several times I *have laid* carpet.

The verbs *rise* and *raise* are also confusing.

Rise is an intransitive verb meaning to go up by itself; it does not take a direct object.

> Today I *rise*. Yesterday I *rose*. Many times I *have risen*.

Raise is a transitive verb meaning to lift something up; it does take a direct object.

> I *raise* my hand each day at school.
> I *raised* my hand yesterday.
> I *have raised* my hand each day this year.

The best thing to do with these confusing verbs is to memorize them and apply them in your everyday conversations.

Self-Test

1. I must have (laid, lain) it in a drawer.

2. Please don't (sit, set) in your fancy clothes.

3. His salary has been (raised, risen) twice, but Alice's hasn't.

4. (Lie, Lay) down, Ralph!

5. I stumbled across the obese men (lying, laying) on the beach.

Answers:

1. laid
2. sit
3. raised
4. Lie
5. lying

PRONOUN CHOICE

Pronouns are words used as substitutes for nouns. Remember, nouns are words that are the names of a subject (person, place, animal, or thing).

We tend to use pronouns to avoid sounding repetitious. Instead of constantly saying someone's name, we may switch to *she* or *he*. It is more polite to use someone's name, but there are times when diverting to pronouns is more appropriate.

>   A parent has many responsibilities. She must provide for all her child's needs.

The pronoun *she* replaces parent.

It requires some thought to know when to use *I* instead of *me*, *she* instead of *her*, *we* instead of *us*, *he* instead of *him*, *they* instead of *them*, and *who* instead of *whom*.

After studying this chapter, it should become more clear when to use which pronoun.

Whom is not used as frequently today as it originally was. There is a clever technique to apply on those questions regarding the correct choice between *who* and *whom* on the ATPE test.

Substitute *he* for *who* and *him* for *whom* with these questions:

>   (Who, whom) did you bring?

Cross out everything up to and including *who, whom*.

>   -- -- -- did you bring?

Begin the question with what is left: Did you bring -- -- --?
   Insert *he* or *him*, whichever fits.

>   Did you bring him?

Remember: *Him* is equivalent to *whom*.

>   Whom did you bring?

Let's try another:

>   (Who, whom) did you say is in the band?
>   Did you say <u>he</u> is in the band?

75   **GRAMMAR**

He = Who:

> Who did you say is in the band?

Who-whom is tested with the part of the sentence that follows them, and not with anything that came before:

> Send it to (whoever, whomever) requests it.

Whoever and *whosoever* are handled the same as *who*. *Whomever* and *whomsoever* are handled the same as *whom*. You would not test that sentence by thinking, "Send it to him." Whatever portion comes before the *who-whom* combination must be crossed out:

> -- -- -- -- -- -- -- requests *it*.
>
> He requests it.

He + *who* = *whoever*:

> Send it to whoever requests it.

The reversal technique can be used with the other combinations of confusing pronouns (I-me, he-him, she-her, we-us, they-them):

> It appears to be (they, them).

Reverse it:

> *They* appear to be it.

Therefore:

> It appears to be *they*.

Sometimes the words *except* and *like* are used as prepositions and require complements:

> Everyone received a gift except me.
> She looks like me.

As and *than* are connectives and introduce clauses:

> He is taller than I.
> I'm as good as he.

The complement of any form of the verb *is* should be in the subject case (I, you, he, she, it, who, we, they).

> The fortunate one was he.
> It could have been my sister and I.

Try to add on to the sentence to figure out the correct pronoun:

> Sally is as tall as (she, her).
> Sally is as tall as (she, her) is tall.

Naturally you would say:

> *She* is tall.
> Sally is as tall as *she*.

The same goes with:

> I'm as good as (he, him).

Add to it:

> I'm as good as (he, him) is good.
> *He* is good.
> I'm as good as *he*.

When you use the word *like*, mentally change the word to *similar to*:

> She looks like (I, me).
> She looks similar to *me*.
> She looks like *me*.

> You're beginning to sound just like (he, him).
> You're beginning to sound similar to *him*.
> You're beginning to sound just like *him*.

Adding on to comparison sentences may not always work:

> You seem to like your cat more than (I, me).

Add to it:

> You seem to like your cat more than *you like me*.

If you use *I* in this sentence, it would mean that you like your pet more than I like your pet. It is unlikely this is how the sentence is to be interpreted.

> You seem to like your cat more than *me*.

Try this one:

> Don't give him more than (I, me).

Add to it:

> Don't give him more than you gave *me*.

Therefore:

> Don't give him more than *me*.

I and *me* are sometimes hard pronouns for students to work with. One technique that helps is to substitute the word *with* for *between*:

> This matter is between you and (I, me).

Cross out the unnecessary words and substitute *with*:

> This matter is with -- (I. me).

You should say: with me.

Therefore: This matter is between you and *me*.

With sentences like this:

> The four of us — George, Fred, Delores, and (I, me) — went to the movie.

Cross out: -- (I, me) went to the movie.

Clearly making it:

> The four of us — George, Fred, Delores, and *I* — went to the movie.

Try this one:

> As for you and (she, her), you can stop trying to aggravate me.

Cross out:

>As for -- (she, her)

You should be saying:

>As for *her* ...

Making it:

>As for you and *her*, you can stop trying to aggravate me.

Practice working out the following exercises to reinforce the new techniques you have just learned.

Self-Test

1. It could have been (I, me).

2. If it had not been (he, him), I would have believed it.

3. Was it (they, them) who left the wine?

4. The fastest runner appears to be (she, her).

Answers:

1. I, 2. he, 3. they, 4. she

POSSESSIVE PRONOUNS

It is important for you to remember that pronouns must agree in number with antecedents:

>Arlene loved *granola bars* and ate *them* often.

>*All* in attendance felt *they* were gypped.

Note: Antecedents are words that refer to nouns or other pronouns already mentioned.

The personal forms of possessive pronouns are: my, your, his, her(s), its, our, your, and their.

The two most troublesome antecedents are: *everybody* and *everyone*.

They are singular but often imply the plural:

> Everyone in the room left his seat.
> Everybody knows her own faults best.

The following chart should refresh your memory on the different forms of pronouns.

PERSON	SUBJECTIVE Singular	Plural	OBJECTIVE Singular	Plural	POSSESSIVE Singular	Plural
First	I	we	me	us	my, mine	our, ours
Second	you	you	you	you	your, yours	your, yours
Third	he	they	him	them	his	their, theirs
	she		her		her, hers	
	it		it		its	
	who	who	whom	whom	whose	whose

We have already reviewed the apostrophe and possession. With pronouns, there are a few more rules to learn:

Do not use the apostrophe with ours, hers, yours, its, theirs, and whose.

Only use an apostrophe with *its* if you mean *it is*.

Be careful not to confuse:

> *you're* with *your* *they're* with *their, there* *who's* with *whose*

Try the following:

> Where do you think (your, you're) going?
>
> (Who's, Whose) coat is that?

Sound out the contractions to make certain you select the correct choice.

> Where do you think you are going?
>
> Whose coat is that?

In none of the possessive forms of the personal pronoun do we use the apostrophe. Remember to keep your pronouns agreeing in number with their antecedents.

ATPE STUDY GUIDE

ADVERBS AND ADJECTIVES

A good way to find out if a word is an adverb or an adjective is to look it up in a current college dictionary.

Once you know whether or not it's an adverb or adjective, you will be able to use it correctly in a sentence.

Adjectives modify nouns; adverbs modify verbs and other modifiers (adjectives, adverbs, clauses, phrases):

> *weak* man (adjective modifying noun *man*)
> *very* weak man (adverb modifying the adjective *weak*)

Many adverbs end in *-ly*—*newly, rarely*—but not all of them do—*rather, very*. There are some adjectives that end in *-ly*—*homely, friendly*—though most do not.

The complement of a verb *to be* may be an adjective describing the subject of the sentence:

> The book is red.

Red modifies *book*, and not the verb *is*. Other verbs (feels, appears, becomes, seems, looks, tastes, sounds, smells, etc.) are similar in function to the verb *to be*.

> The movie is interesting.   The movie sounds interesting.
> The movie seems interesting.

In all these sentences, the complement is an adjective, describing the subject: an interesting movie. A modifier which describes the verb must be an adverb: She sings sweetly. Notice the differences in the following sentences:

> He plays the drum badly. (Badly describes the verb.)
> His playing sounds bad. (Bad describes playing, the subject.)
> The girls sing sweetly.
> The candy tastes sweet.

Self-Test

1. Her secretary was called. He looked (careful, carefully) through the contracts.

2. This isn't poison! Please taste it (confident, confidently).

3. She told me about his misfortune. It sounded (terrible, terribly).

Answers:

1. carefully,   2. confidently,   3. terrible

SENTENCES: COMPLETE AND RUN-ON

A complete sentence contains a subject and a verb. It also expresses a complete thought. It may also be defined as an independent clause. A clause is a group of words containing a subject and a predicate. Remember, the subject is the thing talked about, and a verb or predicate makes a statement about the subject.

In the sentence "The cat chased the rat.", *cat* is the subject, *chased* is the verb, and *rat* is the object. Why do we say this? An action is being performed in the sentence. It is concerned with *chasing*.

> If we ask who or what is performing the action, the answer is *cat* — the subject.

> If we ask what the action is, the answer is *chased* — the verb.

> If we ask who or what is being chased, the answer is *rat* — the object.

In most English sentences, subject precedes verb, and object follows verb.

A run-on sentence does as it implies — it goes on and on. Run-on sentences are ramblers. Consider the following sentence:

> The cat chased the rat and went upstairs to chase the dog and then it ran downstairs to chase the bird and then it went outside to chase the goat and then it decided it was tired and it took a nap, but for only ten minutes, and then it chased the old neighbor lady.

Phew! The cat exhausts the reader. This run-on sentence could be separated into several shorter sentences. Are you able to think of ways to shorten this run-on sentence?

Ideas: The cat chased the rat. The cat went upstairs to chase the dog; then it ran downstairs to chase the bird. It then went outside to chase the goat. Then it decided it was tired, and it took a nap, but for only ten minutes. Then it chased the old neighbor lady.

A run-on sentence is one that follows a preceding sentence as if both were one. There is no period and no capital letter to show the break between them. Some run-on sentences do not interfere with meaning, but they suggest that the writer is illiterate, as our example did.

> Of course we had to go shopping the very first day we discovered more of the virtues of this lovely city.

This sentence leaves the reader in doubt about the intended meaning. The preceding example might be read as one sentence, but what the writer meant was:

> Of course we had to go shopping. The very first day we discovered more of the virtues of this lovely city.

Practice:

Revise these passages to eliminate run-on sentences.

1. Was this the only solution to the dilemma it seems so.

2. A person's character is acquired from his environment he is not born with it.

3. Think what you like I don't care.

Answers:

1. Was this the only solution to the dilemma? It seems so.

2. A person's character is acquired from his environment. He is not born with it.

3. Think what you like. I don't care.

BUILDING/CHANGING SENTENCES: SUBORDINATE AND INVERT

To begin this lesson, it is important you understand the meaning of subordinate.

> subordinate: to place below something else; to make or consider as of lesser value or importance; to make subject.

Any unit with its own subject and predicate is called a clause, but not all clauses are independent–that is, not all clauses can be whole sentences by themselves. Some clauses begin with subordinating conjunctions:

> after, although, as, as if, as though, because, before, even if, even though, how, if, in order that, inasmuch as, provided (that), since, so (that), so...as, so...that, than, that though, unless, until, till, when, whenever, where, wherever, while

When a clause begins with one of these words, it cannot stand alone as a sentence.

Clauses which begin with a relative pronoun (who, whom, which, that) are not whole sentences either. Relative pronouns at the beginning of these clauses indicate that something else is needed to complete the idea so the sentence will make sense.

> Among the sunbathers where the sun shone (fragment)

This fragment may serve as part of a sentence, but not alone as a whole one.

> Among the sunbathers where the sun shone stood a very prosperous junk-food stand.

There are four kinds of subordinating elements which can be used to subordinate a sentence. For example:

> Martha felt rejuvenated after her long jog, and she decided to go out dancing.

Using one of the subordinating conjunctions, you can change it to:

> Since she felt rejuvenated after her long jog, Martha decided to go out dancing.

Using an adjective clause or relative pronoun (who, whom, whose, which, or that), you can change it to:

> Martha, who felt rejuvenated after her long jog, decided to go out dancing.

Beginning a phrase with an -ing verb, you can change it to:

> Feeling rejuvenated after her long jog, Martha decided to go out dancing.

Beginning a phrase with an -ed verb or an adjective, you can change it to:

> Rejuvenated after her long jog, Martha decided to go out dancing. Vigorous after her long jog, Martha decided to go out dancing.

It is best to put the important part of your message in an independent clause and the supporting parts in subordinate elements.

Self-Test

Rewrite the following sentences:

1. Most people are afraid of their first driver's examination, and they are unable to take it with any degree of confidence.
   (Begin with the adjective "afraid.")

2. We filled our glasses and then drank a toast to missed friends.
   (Use "after.")

Answers:

1. Afraid of their first driver's examination, most people are unable to take it with any degree of confidence.

2. After our glasses were filled, we drank a toast to missed friends.

SPELLING

There won't be too many questions regarding spelling on the ATPE, yet it's important to emphasize a few basic rules. Different books will list the fifty words that they think are the most commonly misspelled; unfortunately, very few lists coincide. Here's mine:

succeed, proceed, exceed　　The only words in the entire language ending in *-ceed*.

supersede　　The only word ending in *-sede*.

all right　　Two words, no matter how it is used.

precede, recede, etc.	All other words with a similar-sounding final syllable end *-cede*.
stationery	This is the word that means paper. Notice the *er* in paper.
stationary	The word means standing. Notice the *a* in stand.
separate, comparative	Look for the word *rat* in both.
analyze, paralyze	The only two nontechnical words in the whole language ending in *-yze*.
conscience	Science plus prefix *con-*.

The following list contains words people frequently confuse.

accept, except	To *accept* is to receive willingly. *Except* is to leave out.
affect, effect	To *affect* is to change or influence. To *effect* is to bring about. Effect is also a noun that means **result**.
are, our	*Are* is a verb. *Our* is a possessive pronoun.
break, brake	A *brake* stops a car or a bicycle. To *break* is to separate into parts.
capitol, capital	The *capitol*, a building, is located in the *capital*, a city. *Capital* may also mean money.
complement, compliment	*Complement* is a quantity needed to making a thing complete. To *compliment* is to praise.
conscience, conscious	The *conscience* is the sense of right and wrong. To be *conscious* is to be mentally aware.
council, counsel	A *council* is an assembly or meeting. To *counsel* is to advise.
finally, finely	*Finally* means at the end or at long last. *Finely* means in small pieces.
hear, here	To *hear* is to perceive by the ear. *Here* is the opposite of there.
its, it's	*Its* is the possessive form of it. *It's* is the contraction for **it is**.

passed, past   *Passed* is to go by; to go or allow to go unchallenged; to circulate. *Past* is what has occurred or existed in a period before the present.

peace, piece   *Peace* is the opposite of war. *Piece* is a part of a whole.

principal, principle   A *principal* is the chief administrator of a school. *Principle* is a rule or code of conduct.

stake, steak   A *stake* is driven into the ground. A *steak* is meat.

their, there, they're   *Their* is the possessive form of they. *There* is an adverb of place. *They're* is the contraction for **they are**.

to, too, two   *To* means toward. *Too* means also or indicates more of something than necessary. *Two* is a number.

weather, whether   *Weather* is the outside environment of wind, sun, snow, etc. *Whether* is a conjunction introducing alternatives.

who's, whose   *Who's* is the contraction for **who is**. *Whose* is the possessive form of **who**.

your, you're   *Your* is the possessive form of you. *You're* is the contraction for **you are**.

It would be more time-consuming than useful to continue listing the most commonly misspelled words. The possibilities are limitless. The best thing to do is to incorporate better habits in your daily routine and look up every word you suspect you may be spelling incorrectly.

Self-Test

The ATPE test may include examples like this:

Of the following groups, which word is spelled incorrectly?

1. a. academick
   b. physicist
   c. pharmacist
   d. lecturer

2.   a.   impulsive
      b.   noteworthey
      c.   adaptable
      d.   foreboding

3.   a.   debitt
      b.   liability
      c.   spaghetti
      d.   scrimmage

4.   a.   crevice
      b.   phase
      c.   margin
      d.   overdew

5.   a.   desirable
      b.   favorible
      c.   effective
      d.   embarrassing

Answers:

1. **a.** The correct spelling is *academic*.
2. **b.** The correct spelling is *noteworthy*.
3. **a.** The correct spelling is *debit*.
4. **d.** The correct spelling is *overdue*.
5. **b.** The correct spelling is *favorable*.

Other Educational Resources from
PRIMER PUBLISHERS

EASY FIELD GUIDE SERIES:
- illustrated guides on Arizona and southwestern topics
- pocket-size is convenient for the classroom or in the field
- excellent for both primary and secondary levels
- only $1.25 each

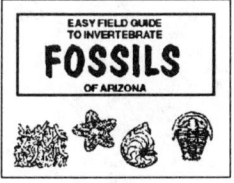
AZ FOSSILS
ISBN 0-935810-57-9

AZ MAMMALS
ISBN 0-935810-16-1

AZ TREES
ISBN 0-935810-18-8

AZ DINOSAURS
ISBN 0-935810-63-3

DESERT BIRDS
ISBN 0-935810-13-7

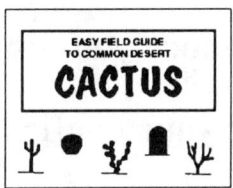
DESERT CACTUS
ISBN 0-935810-15-3

DESERT INSECTS
ISBN 0-935810-14-5

SW NIGHT SKY
ISBN 0-935810-62-5

SW PETROGLYPHS
ISBN 0-935810-60-9

SW ROCK ART
ISBN 0-935810-58-7

SW SNAKES
ISBN 0-935810-17-X

Other suggested titles:

DESERT SURVIVAL HANDBOOK by Charles A. Lehman - Provides basic survival skills necessary to deal with emergencies in the desert. Ideal adjunct text for a unit of instruction on the desert.
ISBN: 0-935810-34-X $5.95

GRAND CANYON RAILROAD by Rudy J. Gerber - A fully illustrated guide to the railroad's history, scenery, ghost towns, wildlife, volcanoes and equipment. Filled with maps and illustrations.
ISBN: 0-935810-44-7 $5.95

FINDING GOLD IN THE DESERT by Otto E. Lynch - Describes techniques of finding, identifying and extracting gold from the deserts of the Southwest.
ISBN: 0-935810-53-6 $4.95

PLACE NAMES IN ARIZONA by Charles H. Newton - From Goldroad, Flagstaff and Window Rock to Tombstone, Snowflake and Mesa, explains how places around the state were named.
ISBN: 0-935810-51-X $3.95

Contact your local bookstore to order these titles.

TESTING NOTES

✓ Get a good night's sleep.

✓ Wear comfortable clothes.

✓ Eat before you test.

✓ Bring your confirmed registration.

✓ Bring photo identification.

✓ Bring two number 2 pencils.

✓ Arrive at the test site early.

✓ Read the questions carefully.

✓ Mark your answer sheet carefully.

✓ Answer all the questions.

✓ Know what to expect.
(study this workbook)